TIME FOR KIDS®

Prepare for TAKS
Nonfiction Reading

Grade 2

TCM 8852

- Culturally diverse text
- Literary elements
- Analysis strategies
- Critical-thinking skills

Teacher Created Materials, Inc.

Editor-in-Chief
Sharon Coan, M.S. Ed.

Art Coordinator
Kevin Barnes

Cover Production
CJae Froshay

Art Director
CJae Froshay

Imaging
Craig Gunnell

Product Manager
Phil Garcia

Publishers
Rachelle Cracchiolo, M.S. Ed.
Mary Dupuy Smith, M.S. Ed.

Articles courtesy of TIME For Kids ©
magazine
TIME For Kids is a registered
trademark of Time Inc.

Authors

Maria Montoya-Hoherstein, Ed.D.

Dixie Bailey Huckabee

Kimberly Royal

Teacher Created Materials, Inc.
6421 Industry Way
Westminster, CA 92683
www.teachercreated.com.
ISBN-0-7439-8652-0
©2004 Teacher Created Materials, Inc.
Made in U.S.A.

Table of Contents

Introduction 5

Science

A Fall from Space 6

Digging Up Dinosaurs 8

Fast, Faster, Fastest! 10

Life in the Desert 12

Life on the Galapagos Islands 14

Zoos with the most Species 16

A Close Look at the Solar System 18

The Case of the Missing Monkey 20

The Solar System 22

Find the Sweet Spot 24

A Garden From Mars 26

Be a Science Spy 28

10 Tips to Stay Safe All Year Round 30

Telescopes 32

Cleaning Up the Water 34

Social Studies

Helping Kids Learn: Egypt 36

The Tallest U.S. Presidents 38

Champion Basketball Player 40

National Treasures 42

Kids Help the Hungry 44

Help for the Helpers 46

Mighty Alaska 48

Sports and People 50

Top 5 Largest Libraries 52

The World's Coral Reefs 54

Fantasy on Ice 56

Choosing Our Leaders 58

Time To Celebrate! 60

The Star-Spangled Banner 62

People Around the World 64

Table of Contents (cont.)

Language Arts

Web Page 66

Dear Aunt Mary and Uncle George 68

By George, It's a Brand New book! 70

Who Turned Off the Lights? 72

A Diary From Long Ago 74

Up, Up, and Away! 76

The Daily Squawker 78

www.exploringnonfiction.com 80

A Busy New President 82

Walt Disney 84

Summer of the Shark 86

The Daily News 88

Back Off, Bullies! 90

Planting Corn 92

Wearing a Helmet Is Cool 94

Math

Top 5 Ice Cream Flavors 96

Using Your Noodle 98

A Day at the Zoo 100

A Time Line of Toys 102

Some Monster Planets! 104

Money and the Price of Things 106

Table of Contents 108

Road Runner Bus Co. 110

Paid to Play Games 112

The Big Game 114

Captain Bob's Seafood Restaurant 116

The Rising Price of Fuel 118

Sydney's Sewer Snapper 120

The New Math: Problems, Problems 122

A Sign of Hope 124

Answer Key 126

Introduction

The articles in *Prepare for TAKS: Nonfiction Reading* provide opportunities for students to interact with authentic, culturally diverse written text. However, exposure to authentic text alone may not be sufficient to prepare students for high-stakes tests. Students need many opportunities in the classroom to encounter the types of questions for which they will be held accountable on state tests.

To meet this need, TAKS-style questions for each article were developed by Texas teachers. These practice questions were patterned after the questions found in the *TAKS Information Booklet* published by the Texas Education Agency (TEA). These questions will give students the opportunity to practice showing their comprehension of text in the TAKS test format. These TAKS-specific questions will allow teachers a "dip stick" to be used with each card to continually monitor a student's comprehension. In essence, each article carries with it a "mini-TAKS." Continuous practice and progress monitoring will aid both students and teachers as they prepare to meet the challenge of a rigorous assessment.

The TEKS student expectations in reading for grades 3-8 are grouped under four umbrella TAKS objectives. These are identified in TEA's *TAKS Reading Information Booklet* as follows:

Objective 1: The student will demonstrate a basic understanding of culturally diverse written texts.

Objective 2: The student will apply knowledge of literary elements to understand culturally diverse texts.

Objective 3: The student will use a variety of strategies to analyze culturally diverse written texts.

Objective 4: The student will apply critical-thinking skills to analyze culturally diverse written texts.

Each article has four questions, in most cases one from each of the four TAKS reading objectives. However, because of the expository nature of the text, there are instances where literary elements (objective 2) are not present. In those instances, a question from another objective is substituted.

How to Use the TAKS Practice Pages

Reproduce the articles and TAKS practice pages. Sometimes have students complete the page on their own for use as a comprehension assessment. At other times, complete the page together, modeling and discussing the test-taking strategies that might be used to answer the questions. With on-going, consistent practice students will become comfortable with the format and perform successfully when they take the TAKS.

A Fall From Space

Russian Space Station Crashes in Pacific Ocean

By Martha Pickerill

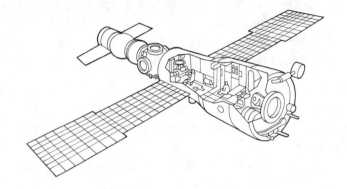

1   (MOSCOW, Russia, March 23) *Mir* went far. *Mir* was a Russian space station. It had been circling the Earth for 15 years. But it had become old and worn out. Astronauts were no longer safe on board the space station. So scientists decided to let it fall from orbit. But they did not let it crash just anywhere. Experts in Russia controlled *Mir*'s fall. On March 22 pieces of the giant spacecraft splashed into the Pacific Ocean. No one was harmed.

Living on Mir

2   *Mir* was once a big part of the Russian space program. Astronauts from the U.S. and many other countries worked on board Mir. The Russian crew lived on *Mir* for a long time. They set records for staying in space 437 straight days. Living on *Mir* taught scientists how to live on the International Space Station.

Near Disaster

3   *Mir* weighed 135 tons. It was the largest human-made object ever brought down from space. Experts said most of the station would burn up when it hit the Earth's atmosphere. But people in Japan were still nervous. Japan was the last country *Mir* would fly over before crashing. But people in Japan had nothing to worry about. This crash was a big success.

❶ Objective 1

This article is mainly about—

Ⓐ how Mir looks.

Ⓑ Mir falling.

Ⓒ people living on Mir.

Ⓓ the building of Mir.

❷ Objective 2

In paragraph 1, the word <u>circling</u> means—

Ⓐ drawing shapes.

Ⓑ living a long time.

Ⓒ having a hard time.

Ⓓ going around.

❸ Objective 3

What is the title of this article?

Ⓐ *Living on Mir*

Ⓑ *A Fall From Space*

Ⓒ *Near Disaster*

Ⓓ *By Martha Pickerill*

❹ Objective 4

In the last paragraph, the author states "This crash was a big success," because—

Ⓐ people watched.

Ⓑ people had a party.

Ⓒ people weren't hurt.

Ⓓ people fell.

Digging Up Dinosaurs

The Creatures of the Red Island

What Weird Teeth!

1   Dinosaur hunters were digging on Madagascar, a nation called the Great Red Island. It is located off the east coast of Africa. They found the lower jaw of an animal with sharp teeth. The teeth stuck out like hooks.

Fascinating Fossils

2   The leader of the dino dig was David Krause. He and his team thought the bone belonged to a crocodile or a flying reptile. The scientists made many trips to Madagascar. On each trip they found more of the creature's bones. It was like putting a puzzle together. The scientists finally decided the bones were from a dinosaur. It probably speared fish and insects with its hook-like teeth.

More Bones

3   Many very old fossils have been found in Madagascar. One dinosaur fossil was 230 million years old. It is the oldest known dinosaur fossil.

4   Scientists have much to learn about dinosaur life. That's why they keep returning to the Red Island. They think its fossils may teach them a lot about this lost world.

How Fossils Form

Dinosaur bones like the ones David Krause found are actually fossils. Here's how a fossil gets formed:

1. To become a fossil, a dead animal must be quickly buried by sand or covered by mud. Otherwise, the body will rot, or it will be torn apart by other animals.

2. Over time, the body of the animal becomes covered by more and more dirt. All the soft parts of the body fall apart. The only things that remain are the bones and teeth.

3. Over millions of years, water filled with minerals seeps into the bone. The minerals slowly replace the chemicals in the bone. These minerals make the bone rock-like. The bone is now a fossil.

1
Objective 1

Paragraph 3 is mainly about—

(A) the shape of bones.

(B) living in Madagascar.

(C) an island.

(D) the age of bones.

2
Objective 2

Look at the pictures of these shapes.

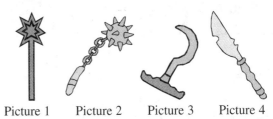

Picture 1   Picture 2   Picture 3   Picture 4

Which shape is most like the tooth described in paragraph 2?

(A) Picture 1

(B) Picture 2

(C) Picture 3

(D) Picture 4

3
Objective 3

What is the title of this article?

(A) *More Bones*

(B) *Digging Up Dinosaurs*

(C) *Paleontology*

(D) *Fossils*

4
Objective 4

The author organizes the section "How Fossils Form," by—

(A) listing steps of how bones become fossils.

(B) telling what a dinosaur looks like

(C) labeling body parts of a dinosaur.

(D) listing the fossils found.

FAST, FASTER, FASTEST!

¹ Imagine that you are at the top of a fast slide. Whoosh! Down you go. Now, you are at the top of a different slide. You push off, and—no whoosh. You slowly inch your way down to the bottom. Why? This experiment will give you the answer.

You Need
- two rulers with a flat side
- two quarters
- several books
- small lump of clay

You Do

1. Stack books 5 inches high.

2. Place one ruler and a lump of clay as shown in the picture. This is your control slide. It will always stay the same.

3. Now set up a second slide with a taller pile of books.

4. Place a quarter at the top of each slide. Let them both go at exactly the same time. Do it yourself, or do it with a friend. Which coin reaches the bottom first?

5. Make the second pile of books even taller. Do step 4 again. Does a steeper slope make a difference?

The Results

The word *slope* means *the slant of an object*. The steeper the slope of an object, the more nearly straight up and down it is. The quarter racing down the steeper slope will reach the bottom faster. The steeper the slope, the faster the fall.

❶ Objective 1

The article is mainly about—

Ⓐ testing slope.

Ⓑ playing with clay.

Ⓒ sliding down slides.

Ⓓ stacking books.

❷ Objective 2

According to the article what happens between setting up the first slide and letting the quarter go?

Ⓐ count the coins

Ⓑ make a ball of clay

Ⓒ make a second slide

Ⓓ do it again

❸ Objective 3

Why does the author set up a control slide?

Ⓐ to tease the loser

Ⓑ to use more books

Ⓒ to compare

Ⓓ to make more fun

❹ Objective 4

The author organizes the bottom section by—

Ⓐ numbering books needed for the experiment.

Ⓑ listing new ideas.

Ⓒ making clay.

Ⓓ telling steps of the experiment.

LIFE IN THE DESERT

How Animals Survive

1   A desert is a place where almost no rain falls. You might not think anything can live there. But many animals call the desert home. They have special bodies and ways of behaving that let them live in these dry, hot places.

2   Desert animals do a good job of staying out of the heat. Many animals move around only at dusk and dawn. For example, some birds are active early in the morning and around sunset, when it is cooler. The rest of the day, they hang out in the shade. Other animals, such as bats, only come out at night. These animals are called nocturnal (knock-turn-uhl).

Keeping Cool

3   Many desert animals have built-in ways to stay cool. For example, some lizards have longer-than-normal legs. These keep their bodies farther from the hot ground. A few animals have extra-long ears. Blood vessels in the ears let out lots of heat, cooling the animal.

Saving Water

4   In the dry desert finding water is hard. Many animals get water from plants, like cacti. The leaves, fruit, and sap hold lots of liquid. Some animals have special ways to recycle the water they have swallowed.

Word Watch

nocturnal—active during the night

cacti—plants with scales or spines instead of leaves, found in dry areas

blood vessels—the tubes that carry blood through a body

recycle—to reuse something

❶ Objective 1

Which of the following is the best summary for this article?

Ⓐ Many animals live in the desert. These animals need to stay cool. They eat cactus.

Ⓑ The desert has very little water. The animals need to find water in plants. Some of the animals know how to reuse water.

Ⓒ Many animals live in the desert even though it is hot. These animals have ways of staying cool. They also have ways of finding water.

Ⓓ Animals in the desert have ways to stay cool. Some lizards have longer legs. Some animals have longer ears to let out heat.

❷ Objective 2

Paragraph 3 is mainly about—

Ⓐ blood in legs.

Ⓑ long legs on bats.

Ⓒ water in plants.

Ⓓ ways to stay cool.

❸ Objective 3

Look at the diagram below.

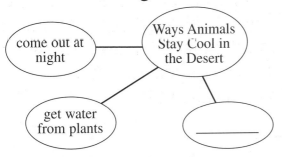

Which idea belongs in the blank?

Ⓐ blood vessels in ears let out heat

Ⓑ cacti have spines

Ⓒ no rain falls

Ⓓ hot, dry place

❹ Objective 4

How does the author organize the section "Word Watch?"

Ⓐ listing plants

Ⓑ defining words

Ⓒ listing traits

Ⓓ telling about animals

Life on the Galapagos Islands

1   The Galapagos Islands are amazing. They are home to some of the most unusual plants and animals in the world. Most of the lizards and insects there and about half the birds and plants are found only on these islands. The Galapagos are 600 miles from Ecuador, a nation in South America.

2   The government of Ecuador wanted to protect the wildlife of the Galapagos. So they made most of the islands a national park. But the wildlife there is still in some danger. An oil spill harmed some of the animals. Pollution is also a problem.

	ANIMAL	FACT	FOOD	THREAT
	Galapagos land iguana	Cousins of the seagoing iguanas, found only on the Galapagos Islands	Plants	Dogs and pollution, both brought in by humans
	Galapagos penguin	The only type of penguin that lives in the northern hemisphere (above the equator)	Fish	Pollution
	Galapagos finch	There are 13 kinds of Galapagos finches. Each has a differently shaped beak.	Insects	Pollution
	Giant tortoise	Huge tortoises, four feet long	Plants	Goats, burros, rats, pollution, and illegal hunting—all brought in by humans

❶ **Objective 1**

Paragraph 2 is mainly about—

(A) the national park.

(B) people throwing trash.

(C) danger to animals.

(D) islands in the ocean.

❷ **Objective 3**

According to the map in the article the Galapagos Islands are located in—

(A) the Atlantic Ocean.

(B) the Pacific Ocean.

(C) the Indian Ocean.

(D) the Arctic Ocean.

❸ **Objective 3**

Which two animals eat plants?

(A) Tortoise and Iguana

(B) Penguin and Finch

(C) Iguana and Finch

(D) Penguin and Tortoise

❹ **Objective 4**

What can the reader tell about most of the animals on Galapagos Islands?

(A) They are in South America.

(B) They all eat fish and insects.

(C) They all swim in the ocean.

(D) They are found only on the islands.

Top 5 U.S. ZOOS With the Most Species

1   The word zoo is short for zoological garden. A zoo is a garden with animals!

2   The first zoo in the United States opened more than 130 years ago in Philadelphia, Pennsylvania. Now there are many zoos across the country. These zoos have hundreds of types of animals—from the pygmy chimpanzee to the giant panda. Here are the zoos with the most species, or types, of animals.

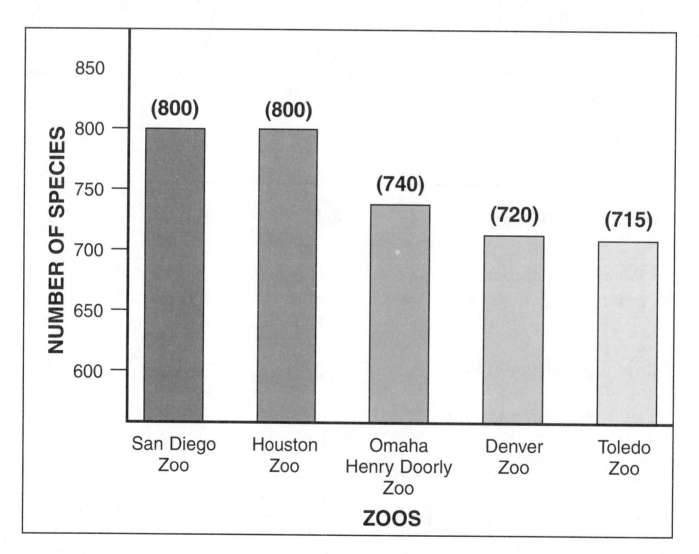

1 Objective 1

Paragraph 1 is mainly about—

(A) a flower garden.

(B) what <u>zoo</u> means.

(C) animals in a garden.

(D) short words.

2 Objective 1

In paragraph 2, which words help the reader know what <u>species</u> means?

(A) *of animals*

(B) *the most*

(C) *the zoos*

(D) *or types*

3 Objective 3

According to the bar graph, which two zoos have the same number of species?

(A) Denver and Omaha

(B) Houston and Toledo

(C) Houston and San Diego

(D) Denver and Toledo

4 Objective 4

The author organizes the bottom section of the article by using—

(A) a bar graph of species at zoos.

(B) a bar graph of popular zoos.

(C) a bar graph of plants in zoos.

(D) a bar graph of people at zoos.

A Close Look at the Solar System

1   Aside from Earth, humans are able to see five planets just by looking up at the night sky. The planets are Mercury, Venus, Mars, Jupiter, and Saturn. To see the three farthest planets—Uranus, Neptune and Pluto—you need to look through a telescope. Telescopes gather light from faraway objects in the sky. They make the objects look brighter and larger. By using powerful telescopes, scientists called astronomers (uh-stron-oh-mers) can study the other eight planets in our solar system. Here is a diagram of our solar system, showing the sun and planets.

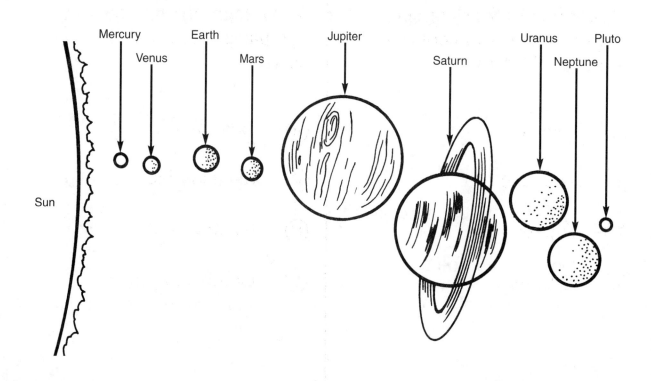

1 **Objective 1**

This article is mainly about—

(A) the order of planets.

(B) the color of planets.

(C) the heat of planets.

(D) the way we see planets.

2 **Objective 2**

According to the article you need a telescope to see the three planets because—

(A) they are far away.

(B) they are bigger.

(C) they are close to us.

(D) they are blue.

3 **Objective 3**

According to the diagram which planet is in between Mars and Saturn?

(A) Venus

(B) Neptune

(C) Jupiter

(D) Uranus

4 **Objective 4**

How might the reader group the planets after reading this article?

(A) close and far away

(B) red and blue

(C) hot and cold

(D) cloudy and ringed

The Case of the Missing Monkey

An African Monkey Has Disappeared Forever

By Elizabeth Siris

1   (WASHINGTON, D.C., September 22) The animal kingdom has lost a member. Scientists say that a West African monkey seems to be extinct. The name of the monkey is Miss Waldron's red colobus. No one has found even one of them in 20 years.

Where Is the Monkey?

2   Like all monkeys, this one is a primate. A primate is a type of animal that includes humans and apes. Primates have advanced brains. They also have fingernails instead of claws. And they have a sense of curiosity. Miss Waldron's red colobus is the first primate to become extinct in hundreds of years.

3   Miss Waldron's red colobus was discovered in 1933. It was named after F. Waldron. She worked for the man who made the discovery. In 1988, the monkey was listed as being in danger of dying out. In 1993, scientists started searching for it. They looked in the rain forests of Ghana and Ivory Coast, two African nations. However, the scientists did not find the loud, 20-pound monkey. They even set up cameras in the jungle to spot one. But none turned up on the film.

Solving the Case

4   Why have the monkeys disappeared? Experts say hunters killed them. It happened because people tore down the monkeys' forest homes. Losing their homes made the monkey easy to find and kill. Scientists hope this loss will cause some good. It may make people want to help other animals in danger of disappearing. Andrew Plumptre works for the U.S. Wildlife Conservation Society. He says, "Africa may seem like a world away. But it's our world, and we need to protect it."

1 Objective 1

Which of the following is the best summary of the article?

(A) Miss Waldron's red colobus is a monkey found by a man in 1933. A lady named Miss Waldron worked for this man. He named the monkey after her.

(B) A monkey has disappeared. This is the first primate to disappear in a hundred years. This monkey lived in Africa.

(C) The Miss Waldron's red colobus has disappeared. No one has found one in 20 years. It is a pretty monkey and people want to find it.

(D) Scientists have been looking since 1993 for the Miss Waldron's red colobus. They looked in two countries. They can't find the monkey.

2 Objective 1

Paragraph 2 is mainly about—

(A) primates that have fingernails.

(B) primates that look like humans.

(C) what a primate is like.

(D) what a primate eats.

3 Objective 3

Look at the diagram below

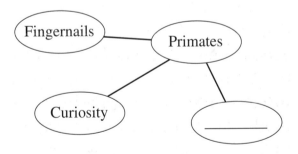

Which idea belongs in the blank?

(A) brain

(B) red

(C) claws

(D) humans

4 Objective 4

The author ends the article with this quote, "Africa may seem like a world away, but it's our world, and we need to protect it," because—

(A) Africa is far away and across an ocean.

(B) animals go back and forth to other countries.

(C) everyone should live in Africa.

(D) everyone is responsible for animals in the world.

The Solar System

1 The solar system is made up of the sun and the objects that orbit around the sun. These objects include the nine planets, asteroids (small rocky objects), and comets (small icy objects).

The Sun

2 The sun has 99 percent of the material, or mass, of the solar system. Its gravity is so strong, it holds together all the objects of the solar system.

The Inner Planets

3 The four inner planets are Mercury, Venus, Earth, and Mars. They are small and rocky. Mercury is closest to the sun and has no atmosphere. Venus's atmosphere keeps in the sun's heat. That's why it is the hottest planet in the solar system. Only Earth has oxygen, water, and life.

The Outer Planets

4 The outer planets are Jupiter, Saturn, Uranus, Neptune, and Pluto. The first four are huge planets made mainly of gas. They all have rings and many moons. Pluto is tiny and rocky. Some scientists consider Pluto a comet, not a planet.

Fascinating Facts

- The sun shines 10 times as strong on Mercury as it does on Earth.
- Some ice chunks in Saturn's rings are as large as a house.
- Uranus is the only planet that spins on its side. Its north and south poles point at the sun.
- A canyon on Mars is as long as the distance between New York and San Francisco.
- The Great Red Spot is a hurricane in the atmosphere of Jupiter. The storm is three times the size of Earth.

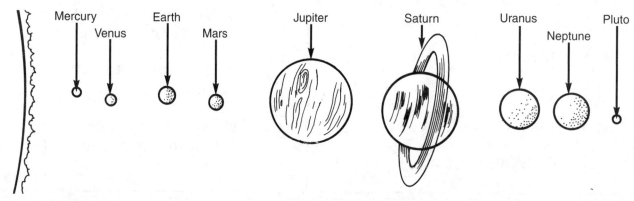

❶   **Objective 1**

In paragraph 1, which words help the reader know what <u>comets</u> mean?

Ⓐ   *small icy objects*

Ⓑ   *include the nine planets*

Ⓡ   *small rocky objects*

Ⓓ   *orbit around the sun*

❷   **Objective 2**

According to the article Venus is the hottest planet because—

Ⓐ   it is a red planet.

Ⓑ   its air keeps in the sun's heat.

Ⓒ   it is small and rocky.

Ⓓ   it is the closest to the sun.

❸   **Objective 3**

Look at the diagram below.

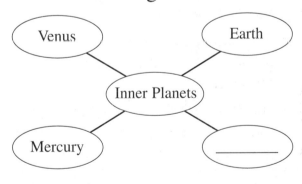

Which idea belongs in the blank?

Ⓐ   Jupiter

Ⓑ   Sun

Ⓒ   Mars

Ⓓ   Uranus

❹   **Objective 4**

The author organizes the section "Fascinating Facts" by—

Ⓐ   listing the planets.

Ⓑ   showing the planets.

Ⓒ   telling the heat of the planets.

Ⓓ   stating facts of the solar system.

FIND THE SWEET SPOT

1   Have you heard of the "sweet spot" on a baseball bat? It is the best place on a bat to hit a ball. Why? Because it will give you the most power with the least effort.

2   How do you find the sweet spot? Take a tip from big league sluggers Sammy Sosa and Barry Bonds. They say you can feel it in your fingertips. Try the science experiment below. Then you will see what they mean!

You Need
- a baseball bat
- a spoon or hammer
- tape

You Do
1. Find a "teammate" to help you.

2. Curl your fingertips around the knob of the bat. (The knob is the bulge at the skinny end of the bat.) Let the bat hang straight down.

3. Ask your teammate to tap on the bat with something hard. (A hammer or heavy spoon would be great.) The tapping should start at the top near the knob. Then it should slowly move down the bat.

4. Feel the bat vibrating between your fingers? At some point in the tapping, you will feel the vibrations almost stop. The sound of the taps may change, too. That's the sweet spot!

5. Use tape to mark where the sweet spot begins and ends.

Why It Happened
A ball flies farther when you hit it on the sweet spot. How come? When your bat hits a ball, the bat vibrates. It does this just as it did when it was tapped by the hammer or spoon. The vibrations move up and down the bat. At the sweet spot, those vibrations run into each other. They cancel each other out.

❶ Objective 1

In step 1, <u>teammate</u> means—

Ⓐ team.

Ⓑ matter.

Ⓒ partner.

Ⓓ reader.

❷ **Objective 3**

What is a heading in the article?

Ⓐ *Find the Sweet Spot*

Ⓑ *Why It Happened*

Ⓒ *Take a tip*

Ⓓ *Sammy Sosa*

❸ **Objective 3**

In the experiment what happens between holding the bat and fccling thc vibrations?

Ⓐ Use tape to mark the spot.

Ⓑ Tap the bat.

Ⓒ Get materials you need.

Ⓓ Hit the ball on the sweet spot.

❹ **Objective 4**

The hitter wants to hit the ball on the sweet spot because—

Ⓐ it has the most power.

Ⓑ it tastes good.

Ⓒ it is the middle of the bat.

Ⓓ it is the smallest part of the bat.

A Garden from Mars

By Kyle Brunson

1   It's an out-of-this-world event! The first Martian vegetables ever grown are now on Earth. The tiny asparagus and potato plants did not arrive on a spaceship. They were grown right here by Michael Mautner. He is a scientist from New Zealand, an island nation in the southern Pacific Ocean. Maurer grew the vegetables on Earth. But the soil came from Mars.

Rocks From Mars

2   How did Mautner get soil from Mars? He made it from two Martian meteorites. These chunks of rock from Mars had landed on Earth. One rock was found in the Sahara Desert in Africa. The other one was found in Antarctica (near the South Pole).

Making Martian Soil

3   Mautner studied the rocks. He found that they had minerals that plants need to grow. "It's as if the Martian soil is naturally fertilized," Mautner explains. (Fertilizer is a substance that helps plants grow.) Mautner cut up the Martian rocks. Then he turned the slices into powder. He mixed the rock powder with water. Then he put tiny bits of asparagus and potato plants into the mixture. In a few weeks the plants grew a couple of inches high.

4   "I was excited to see the vegetables grow so well," Mautner says. "In the future people starting a colony on Mars could grow food there."

❶ Objective 1

Which of the following is the best summary for this article?

(A) Scientist Michael Mautner found rocks from Mars. He made the rocks into dirt and added water. He planted seeds in the dirt.

(B) Scientist Michael Mautner found two rocks from Mars. He found one in the Sahara desert and one in Antarctica. He made the rocks into dirt.

(C) Scientist Michael Mautner grew vegetables on earth in dirt from Mars. This tells us that Mars can grow plants with water. So if people go to Mars they will have food.

(D) Scientist Michael Mautner grew vegetables using dirt from Mars. He grew asparagus and potato plants. The plants grew to be a few inches tall.

❷ Objective 2

In paragraph two, which words help the reader know what meteorites mean?

(A) *chunks of rock*

(B) *landed on Earth*

(C) *found in the desert*

(D) *other one*

❸ Objective 3

Look at the diagram below.

Found rocks → _____ → Crushed rocks

Which idea belongs in the empty box?

(A) Bits of plants

(B) Sliced rocks

(C) Some water

(D) Grow seeds

❹ Objective 4

The author named this article "A Garden from Mars" because—

(A) the vegetables were flown from Mars.

(B) the Martians planted the garden.

(C) the vegetables were planted in the Sahara desert.

(D) the dirt used came from Mars.

Be a Science Spy

1   Many scientists study animals. They do it to understand how the animals act. First, scientists must watch the animals very carefully. Then, they must write down what they see. You can do the same thing scientists do. To learn how, just follow these directions:

1. Choose an animal. It's fun to watch wild animals, like squirrels, rabbits and chipmunks. You can also try watching a pet animal.

2. Make a chart like this on a piece of notebook paper.

MY ANIMAL	HOW OFFEN
Scratched ear	✓✓✓

3. Spend 5 to 10 minutes watching your animal. Make a note on the chart of the first five behaviors you see (scratching behind ear, sneezing, etc.).

4. Each time the animal does one of the behaviors again, make a mark on your chart.

5. Think about which behaviors the animal did most often and which it did least often.

6. Make guesses about which behaviors it will do next.

7. Look at another animal of the same type. For example, watch a different squirrel or a different cat. See if similar animals behave the same way.

1 Objective 1

The article is mainly about—

Ⓐ picking an animal.

Ⓑ how to learn about animals.

Ⓒ how to take notes.

Ⓓ what animals look like.

2 Objective 1

In step 3, which words help the reader know what behaviors mean?

Ⓐ *spend 5 to 10 minutes*

Ⓑ *watching your animal*

Ⓒ *scratching behind ears, sneezing*

Ⓓ *a note on the chart*

3 Objective 3

According to the article what do you do between drawing a chart and writing what you see on the chart?

Ⓐ Watch the animal you picked.

Ⓑ Pick a different animal.

Ⓒ Think about what the animal might do.

Ⓓ Make guesses.

4 Objective 4

The author organizes the section after the 1st paragraph by—

Ⓐ listing animals.

Ⓑ giving meanings of words.

Ⓒ numbering things animals do.

Ⓓ giving steps on what to do.

10 Tips to Stay Safe All Year Round

1   It's fun to play outside. But being outside can sometimes be dangerous. It's important to avoid danger in and out of the house. To do that, you should always be alert and careful. Here are some things you can do to stay safe. How many can you remember?

1. Take a friend with you when you go places or play outside.

2. Know your full name, address, telephone number, and your parents' names.

3. If you ever get lost in a public place, talk to someone in charge right away. He or she will help you find your parents.

4. Before taking anything from anyone, even from someone you know, check with your parents or a grown-up you trust.

5. Check first with your parents or the person in charge before you go anywhere.

6. Say no if someone tries to treat you in a way that makes you confused or scared. Tell your parents or a trusted grown-up right away.

7. Talk with your parents about which online activities are safe and which are not.

8. Use the "buddy" system when you go swimming. Always make sure a trusted grown-up is watching.

9. Always cross a street at a corner or crosswalk. Look left and right before crossing.

10. Whenever you ride in a car, ride in the back seat and buckle up.

1 **Objective 1**

This article is mainly about—

(A) keeping safe inside.

(B) keeping safe outside.

(C) staying out of trouble.

(D) staying in trouble.

2 **Objective 1 (no obj. 2)**

In paragraph 1, the word <u>avoid</u> means—

(A) to go see.

(B) to go inside.

(C) to keep safe.

(D) to keep away from.

3 **Objective 3**

The most likely reason the author wrote this article was to—

(A) show how to play in a park.

(B) explain how to swim.

(C) explain what to do outside to be safe.

(D) show children how to use a car seat.

4 **Objective 4**

The author organizes the bottom part of the article by—

(A) listing rules you follow to stay safe.

(B) numbering steps on how to play at the park.

(C) listing how to learn how to swim.

(D) helping children remember their address.

Telescopes

1   When did the universe begin? Does it Stretch forever? For thousands of years, humans have been watching the heavens and asking questions. Today, most of that watching is done on mountain tops. That's where scientists have been building powerful new telescopes. These telescopes are all over the world, from Hawaii to South America to Europe. New super telescopes are helping us see farther into space than ever before.

It's Done With Mirrors

2   A large telescope's power has to do with mirrors inside it. The bigger the mirror, the more starlight it can collect. Today, new telescopes have giant mirrors. They are controlled by computers. The Keck telescope in Hawaii has a mirror that is 33 feet across!

Close-Up of the Stars

3   Giant telescopes are helping astronomers (uh-stron-oh-mers) make amazing finds. (An astronomer is a scientist who studies outer space.) One astronomer used the Keck telescope to discover 35 planets circling different stars. A new telescope in Chile helped scientists figure out the age of the universe: 14 billion years.

HOW TELESCOPES WORK

There are two kinds of telescopes.

A **refracting telescope** has a big glass lens at the front. It focuses the light from an object. Another lens, called an eyepiece, makes the object look bigger.

A **reflecting telescope** has a curved mirror at one end of it. It focuses the light of an object onto a flat mirror at the other end. This mirror reflects the light into the eyepiece lens.

Most large telescopes are the reflecting kind. That's because mirrors can be made larger than lenses.

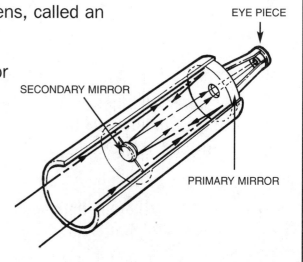

EYE PIECE

SECONDARY MIRROR

PRIMARY MIRROR

---

① Objective 1

Paragraph 2 is mainly about—

Ⓐ   the Keck telescope.

Ⓑ   the state of Hawaii.

Ⓒ   the mirrors in telescopes.

Ⓓ   the starlight in the sky.

② Objective 2

In the article scientists figured out the age of the universe because—

Ⓐ   they were able to use a new telescope.

Ⓑ   they counted the stars in the sky.

Ⓒ   the found 35 planets.

Ⓓ   they counted the planets in the sky.

③ Objective 3

Look at the diagram below

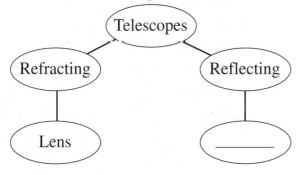

Which idea belongs in the blank?

Ⓐ   Computers
Ⓑ   Mirrors
Ⓒ   Astronomers
Ⓓ   Light

④ Objective 4

The author organizes the section "How Telescopes Work" by—

Ⓐ   telling about stars in the sky.

Ⓑ   telling about planets.

Ⓒ   explaining how a camera lens works.

Ⓓ   describing two kinds of telescopes.

Cleaning Up the Water

In one country in Asia, a dress can help keep people from getting sick.

By Mary Upshaw

This woman is wearing a sari. The sari cloth makes a good water filter.

1   For most Americans, getting a glass of clean water is easy. You can just turn on the tap. But many people around the world drink water straight from rivers and lakes. That can cause big problems.

Dangerous Water

2   One country where some people do not drink from a tap is Bangladesh (bang-gla-DESH), a nation in Asia. There, women collect their family's water from ponds and streams. The brown water is filled with dirt, chemicals, germs, and other gunk. The germs can cause terrible sicknesses, such as cholera (COLL-er-uh).

How to Clean It

3   How is dirty water made clean? Special machines can do the cleaning. But the equipment is very expensive.

4   In Bangladesh, most towns cannot afford the water-cleaning equipment. So scientist Rita Colwell tried to find a simple way to clean water.

A-Dress-ing a Problem

5   Colwell did some experiments with a kind of cloth. The cloth is used to make a colorful dress called a sari (44-ree). The dresses are worn by women in Bangladesh. Colwell folded the dress cloth four times over. She discovered that it made a very good filter. It lets the water pass through, but blocks almost all the dirt and germs.

6   Thanks to a dress, water may be safer to drink in Bangladesh!

① **Objective 1**

According to the article the cloth needed to be folded four times over to—

Ⓐ get more dirt and germs out of the water.

Ⓑ keep women warmer.

Ⓒ give women shade from the sun.

Ⓓ protect a woman's head from the heat.

② **Objective 1**

Read the meanings below for the word <u>tap.</u>

tap (tap) *noun*

1. water faucet **2.** drink that comes from a tap **3.** tool that cuts the screw thread **4.** an electric end

Which meaning best fits the way <u>tap</u> is used in paragraph 1?

Ⓐ Meaning 1
Ⓑ Meaning 2
Ⓒ Meaning 3
Ⓓ Meaning 4

③ **Objective 3**

Look at the diagram below.

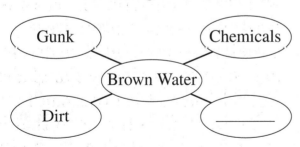

Which idea belongs in the empty circle?

Ⓐ Dresses
Ⓑ Color
Ⓒ Germs
Ⓓ Asia

④ **Objective 4**

Using the sari to filter water is a good thing because—

Ⓐ they are colorful.

Ⓑ they cover the water.

Ⓒ there is water everywhere.

Ⓓ there are a lot of them in Bangladesh.

Helping Kids Learn: Egypt

1   It has been hard for girls to go to school in Egypt (ee-gypt). This is because most people do not live close to schools in that North African nation. Boys can walk miles to schools. But in Egypt, many girls are not allowed to walk far from home—not even to go to school. Also, some families are poor. They cannot pay for books and uniforms for all of their children. So they just spend money on their sons.

UNICEF Helps Out

2   In 1992, the leaders of Egypt asked UNICEF to help. UNICEF stands for United Nations Children's Fund. UNICEF tries to help kids all over the world. In Egypt, UNICEF had an idea: build schools closer to the girls! Also, UNICEF said change class times. This change would let girls do chores at home and still go to school.

New Schools for All

3   The idea worked. Today new schools have been built in more than 2,000 towns and cities around Egypt. In many new schools, there are more girls than boys. In one school the student with the best test scores was a girl!

Fast Facts on Egypt

• The official name of Egypt is the Arab Republic of Egypt.

• Egypt is in the northeast part of Africa. Most of the country is in the desert.

• The Nile River runs through Egypt. It is the world's longest river. Almost everyone in Egypt lives along its banks.

• Egypt's capital city is Cairo (kai row). More than nine million people live there.

• Egyptians speak a language called Arabic.

1 **Objective 3**

What is the title of this article?

Ⓐ *Schools and Education*

Ⓑ *Helping Kids Learn: Egypt*

Ⓒ *UNICEF Helps Out*

Ⓓ *Fast Facts on Egypt*

2 **Objective 2**

What is the main problem in the article?

Ⓐ Girls have lower test scores than boys.

Ⓑ Girls are not going to school.

Ⓒ Children in Egypt do not speak English.

Ⓓ Egypt is mostly desert.

3 **Objective 3**

Read this diagram of information from the article.

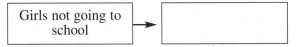

Which idea belongs in the empty box?

Ⓐ Give fewer chores to girls so that they can go to school.

Ⓑ UNICEF pays for books and uniforms for all the children.

Ⓒ In many new schools there are more girls than boys.

Ⓓ Build more than 2000 new schools close to where the girls live.

4 **Objective 4**

The author organizes *Fast Facts on Egypt* by—

Ⓐ listing information about the country in the article.

Ⓑ explaining the difference between Egypt and other Arab countries.

Ⓒ showing why girls should go to school.

Ⓓ telling the reader about Egypt's landforms.

The TALLEST U.S. Presidents

[1] Presidents come in all different sizes. The shortest president ever was James Madison. He was 5 feet, 4 inches tall. But several of our presidents were more than 6 feet tall. Size up the tallest of our leaders. Here is a graph of the tallest U.S. presidents.

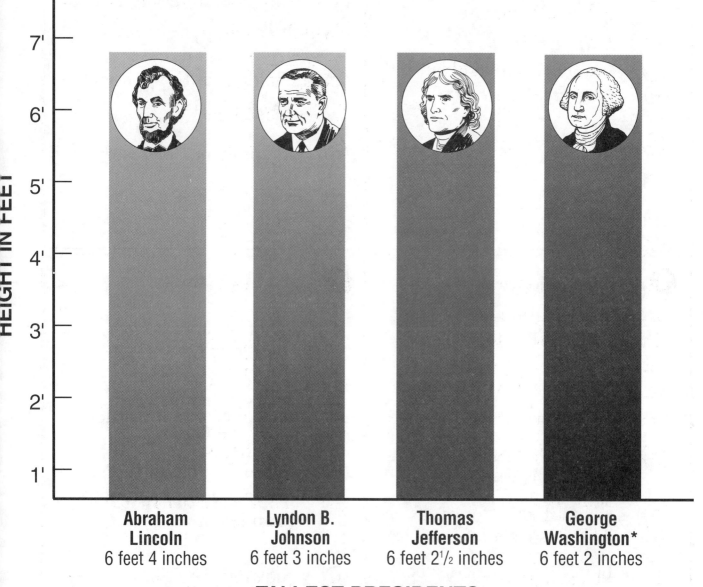

HEIGHT IN FEET

Abraham Lincoln	Lyndon B. Johnson	Thomas Jefferson	George Washington*
6 feet 4 inches	6 feet 3 inches	6 feet 2½ inches	6 feet 2 inches

TALLEST PRESIDENTS

* George Washington is tied with four other presidents. They are Chester A. Arthur, Franklin D. Roosevelt, George Bush, Bill Clinton.

❶ Objective 1

This article is mainly about—

(A) Abraham Lincoln.

(B) the presidents having the greatest height.

(C) the shortest president ever.

(D) presidents of all different sizes.

❷ Objective 1

Read the meaning below for the word <u>tie</u>.

> **tie** (tï) *verb*
>
> **1.** to secure with a rope. **2.** to knot string or laces **3.** to form a knot **4.** to be equal in points

Which meaning best fits the way <u>tied</u> is used in the last paragraph?

(A) Meaning 1

(B) Meaning 2

(C) Meaning 3

(D) Meaning 4

❸ Objective 3

From what the reader learns about the U.S. presidents, which statement would NOT be reasonable?

(A) There were several presidents that were the same height.

(B) The shortest U.S. president was 5 feet 4 inches tall.

(C) The tallest U.S. president was Abraham Lincoln.

(D) Only George Washington was 6 feet 2 inches tall.

❹ Objective 4

How are the men in the pictures alike?

(A) They were tall presidents.

(B) They were our first presidents.

(C) They wrote the Constitution.

(D) They freed the slaves.

Chamique Holdsclaw: Champion Basketball Player

By Curtis Slepian

1   Chamique (Shuh-MEEK-waw) Holdsclaw became interested in hoops almost by accident. She was born in 1972 in New York City. When Chamique was 11, her parents broke up and she went to live with her grandmother. She hung out with her cousin. He liked to play basketball every day at the playground. Chamique watched the boys play. When they finished, she decided to play by herself. One day the boys invited her to play. She was good!

Winning Championships

2   Chamique got even better with practice. She led her high school team to four New York State hoop titles. Then she went to the University of Tennessee.

3   With Chamique, Tennessee won three straight women's national championships. Chamique was an All-American every year. She was College Player of the Year for three years.

On to the Pros

4   Chamique graduated from college in 1998. Some people call her the female Michael Jordan.

She even wears his number: 23. She was drafted by the Washington (D.C.) Mystics of the Women's National Basketball Association (WNBA). Playing at forward, Chamique was voted the league's Rookie of the Year.

Playing for the U.S.A.

5   Chamique has also played for her country. In 1998, she won a gold medal at the World Championships. She was picked for the USA 2000 Olympic basketball team.

6   Chamique is proud of being a role model to girls. But to her, the most important thing is "to make your family proud." She has done that!

❶ **Objective 1**

Paragraphs 2 and 3 are mostly about—

Ⓐ Chamique's time with her grandmother.

Ⓑ Chamique meeting Michael Jordan.

Ⓒ Chamique being a role model.

Ⓓ Chamique winning when she was in school.

❷ **Objective 2**

How did Chamique become interested in basketball?

Ⓐ She watched her cousin and his friends.

Ⓑ She learned from her grandmother.

Ⓒ She met Michael Jordan.

Ⓓ She went to an Olympic training camp.

❸ **Objective 3**

Read the chart below. It shows the order in which some events happened in the article.

She played with a high school team.
↓
She won 3 national championships.
↓
↓
Chamique graduated from college.

Which of these belongs in the empty box?

Ⓐ She was College Player of the Year.

Ⓑ She lived with her grandmother.

Ⓒ She wore number 23.

Ⓓ She was voted Rookie of the Year.

❹ **Objective 4**

Which sentence from the article shows the reader that people think Chamique plays well?

Ⓐ *Then she went to the University of Tennessee.*

Ⓑ *Chamique is proud of being a role model to girls.*

Ⓒ *Some people call her a female Michael Jordan.*

Ⓓ *She hung out with her cousin.*

CHAPTER 9

NATIONAL TREASURES
History of the National Parks

1   The United States has many national parks. A national park is a large piece of land owned by the U.S. government. National parks take up almost 81 million acres of land. The park system includes battlefields, monuments, memorials, military parks, and other places.

A Man with a Dream

2   George Catlin came up with the idea of a national park. He was an American artist. He loved the beautiful land in the West. He was afraid it would be ruined when settlers moved in. So, in 1832, he wrote that this wild country should be left alone. That way the land would stay wild and beautiful forever.

The First National Park

3   Forty years later, Catlin's great idea came true. In 1872, the first national park was named. It was called Yellowstone National Park. Many more parks were created, including Yosemite, Mammoth Cave, and Zion. Park rangers protect these national treasures.

This Land Is Your Land

There are 364 places in the national park system. They are found across the U.S. Here are just a few of them.

Hawaii Volcanoes National Park
(Near Hilo, Hawaii)

Visitors can see Mauna Loa, the world's biggest volcano. It is 13,677 feet high.

Grand Canyon National Park
(Arizona)

This amazing canyon was made by the Colorado River. At one point, it is 6,000 feet from the top to the bottom.

Cape Cod National Seashore
(Wellfleet, Massachusetts)

This park includes a 40-mile beach along the Atlantic Ocean. There are also two famous old lighthouses. They are named the Nauset Light and the Highland Light.

Objective 1

1

Read the first sentence of the summary below.

Summary of "National Parks"

George Catlin was afraid the country's land would be ruined.

Which of the following completes the summary above?

- (A) He wrote about the need to save the West. He loved the West.
- (B) His dream of saving the wild country came true when the first national park was named. Now, there are many more national parks.
- (C) Forty years later, the first national park was named Yellowstone. It is the biggest park in the world.
- (D) So, the U.S. government set aside parks for the military to use. Later, Mammoth Cave became a national park.

Objective 2

2

What is the main problem in the article?

- (A) Many settlers were moving West and could ruin the land.
- (B) American artists were unable to paint the colors of the West.
- (C) The U.S. government did not want any national parks.
- (D) The Colorado River does not accept motorboats.

Objective 3

3

What happened after many parks were created?

- (A) They were named after famous people.
- (B) George Catlin wrote about them.
- (C) The first national park was named.
- (D) They were protected by park rangers.

Objective 4

4

Read the headlines of these newspaper articles.

American Artists are the Best!	Come Settle the West!	Save Our Treasures!	Join the Military!
1	2	3	4

Which newspaper story did Catlin most likely write?

- (A) Headline 1
- (B) Headline 2
- (C) Headline 3
- (D) Headline 4

Kids Help the Hungry

A brother and sister remember others on Thanksgiving.

1   (BOSTON, Massachusetts, November 22) Danny and Betsy Nally like to talk turkey. They also like hungry people to eat turkey. This brother and sister team are helping to give turkeys to the poor on Thanksgiving.

Helping the Poor

2   Danny got the idea to feed hungry people in 1996. That's when he learned that thousands of people in Massachusetts would not have a Thanksgiving turkey. "I felt that was very wrong," Daniel, age 13, said. So he and Betsy, age 11, went around their neighborhood. They were looking for people who wanted to give away turkeys. "My sister and I printed up some flyers asking for donations," said Danny. "And then we went around my neighborhood giving them out."

Handing Out Turkeys

3   Daniel and Betsy went on to start Turkeys R Us. Over the years, they have given more than 3,000 turkeys to the Greater Boston Food Bank. That's a group that gives food to the hungry. Picking up the turkeys has not been easy. Their parents have helped the kids lift the frozen turkeys onto trucks. They also drove the turkeys to the Greater Boston Food Bank.

4   This year the Nallys hope to give away 4,000 birds. "Our big goal is to end hunger one step at a time," Danny says.

1 Objective 1

Read the meaning below for the word <u>step</u>.

> **step** (step) *noun*
> **1.** a way of walking **2.** a footprint **3.** stair **4.** an action to achieve a goal

Which meaning best fits the way <u>step</u> is used in the last paragraph?

(A) Meaning 1

(B) Meaning 2

(C) Meaning 3

(D) Meaning 4

2 Objective 2

Why are Danny and Betsy collecting turkeys?

(A) to start their own store

(B) to feed people in their neighborhood

(C) to help end hunger

(D) to let the wild turkeys go

3 Objective 3

What is the subtitle to this article?

(A) *Kids Help the Hungry*

(B) *Thanks to Danny and Betsy, many people have a happy Thanksgiving.*

(C) *A brother and sister remember others on Thanksgiving.*

(D) *(BOSTON, Massachusetts, November 22)*

4 Objective 4

Which statement is true of Daniel and Betsy's parents?

(A) They helped with the project.

(B) They cannot lift heavy turkeys.

(C) They stayed away from the project.

(D) They live in Texas.

Help for the Helpers

By Martha Pickerill

1   David Krause is a scientist. He searches for dinosaur fossils. In 1996, Krause was digging for dinosaur bones in Madagascar (mad-uh-GAS-car). Madagascar is an island near the east coast of Africa. While Krause dug, kids from the area helped him. They told Krause where to hunt for fossils.

2   Krause was happy for their help. But he wondered why the children weren't in school. Krause found that the kids had no school. Their village was too poor to build one. Krause wanted to pay back the village people for their kindness. So he and other Americans hired a teacher for the village.

Back in the Village

3   In 1998, Krause came back to the village. He found that 60 kids, ages 5 to 17, were in school. Krause wanted to do even more for the village. He started the Madagascar Ankizy Fund to raise money. (Ankizy means children in the local language.) The fund did a good job. In 1999, it paid for a new schoolhouse. It also paid for another teacher. Soon, the village will have a new well. It will give people clean water.

More Work to Do

4   Krause visits schools in the U.S. He talks about his work in Madagascar and the village. After hearing him, many students are raising money. Krause says this money will help "the lives of kids on the other side of the planet."

1 **Objective 1**

In paragraph 3, which words help the reader know what <u>fund</u> means?

(A) *good job*

(B) *paid for*

(C) *new schoolhouse*

(D) *will have*

2 **Objective 2**

Which of these best describes how Krause felt toward the children?

(A) grateful

(B) nervous

(C) angry

(D) lonely

3 **Objective 3**

What happens after Krause finds out the children don't have a school?

(A) He builds a new well.

(B) He becomes a scientist.

(C) He digs for fossils.

(D) He hires a teacher.

4 **Objective 4**

What will probably happen to the village in the future?

(A) The people in the village will tell Krause to leave.

(B) The village will close the school.

(C) The people in the village will better their lives.

(D) The children will move to the U.S.

Mighty Alaska

1   Alaska is very far north. So it is cold and snowy much of the year. The capital city of Alaska is Juneau (june-o). Alaska is one of the biggest states in the U.S. Even its mountains are big. Mount McKinley, the tallest peak in the U.S., is 20,329 feet high.

2   Alaska has many natural resources. For example, the Gulf of Alaska is full of fish. Alaska also has a lot of oil. Many oil wells are located in Prudhoe Bay. About one-fifth of all oil used in the U.S. comes from Prudhoe Bay.

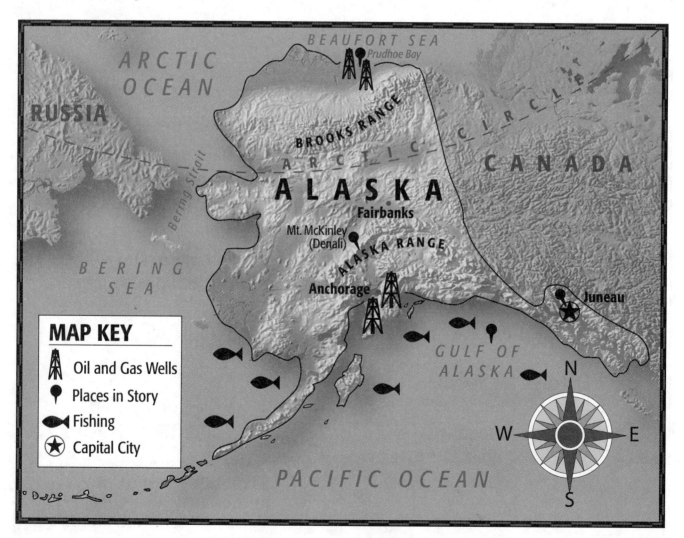

MAP KEY
- Oil and Gas Wells
- Places in Story
- Fishing
- Capital City

❶ **Objective 1**

Paragraph 2 is mostly about—

(A) the fish found in Alaska.

(B) Alaska being near Prudoe Bay.

(C) how to find oil in Alaska.

(D) Alaska being a rich land.

❷ **Objective 2**

Why is Alaska so cold and snowy?

(A) It sits on a tall mountain.

(B) It gets cold waves from the Pacific Ocean.

(C) It is very far north.

(D) It is so big.

❸ **Objective 3**

According to the map, where are Alaska's oil and gas wells?

(A) north

(B) north and south

(C) east

(D) east and west

❹ **Objective 4**

The author organizes paragraphs 1 and 2 by—

(A) explaining what makes Alaska special.

(B) showing how close Alaska is to Russia.

(C) comparing Alaska to other states.

(D) telling a story about how Alaska became a state.

SPORTS AND PEOPLE
The History of the Olympics

The First Olympics

1   The next summer Olympic Games will be held in Athens, Greece, in 2004. Greece is where the very first Olympic Games were held. They took place almost 3,000 years ago in Olympia, Greece. They were started to honor Zeus, a Greek god. In those days, star athletes didn't win gold medals. Instead, they won crowns made of olive leaves. Only men took part. Women could not even see the events. The ancient Games took place until about 400 a.d. That's when a Roman emperor ended them.

The Modern Games

2   After about 1,500 years, the Olympics Games began again. The first modern Games were held in Athens, Greece, in 1896. The next Games took place in 1900. In those Games, women were allowed to take part in three sports. Today more than a third of all Olympic athletes are women!

3   The Olympic symbol is five rings that are connected. Each ring stands for a continent. In 1920 an Olympic flag first showed the rings. It also had the Olympic motto: Faster, Higher, Stronger.

Facts From the 2000 Olympics

- Australia built the largest Olympic Stadium ever. Four jumbo jet planes could fit side by side in it.

- More than 60,000 meals a day were served to athletes and other people at the Sydney Games.

- The youngest Sydney Games athlete (at age 13) was Faithimath Fariha. This swimmer is from an island nation called the Maldives.

---

❶ Objective 1

Why were the Olympic Games first started?

Ⓐ   to win medals

Ⓑ   to honor women

Ⓒ   to honor Zeus

Ⓓ   to honor a Roman leader

❷ Objective 2

Why is Greece important to the Olympic Games?

Ⓐ   It is where they love gold medals.

Ⓑ   It is where olives are grown.

Ⓒ   It is where women started playing in the Olympics.

Ⓓ   It is where the first Olympics Games were held.

❸ Objective 3

Look at the diagram about the first Olympics and the modern Olympics.

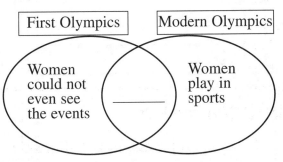

First Olympics   Modern Olympics

Women could not even see the events   Women play in sports

Which of the following belongs in the blank?

Ⓐ   First held in Athens, Greece
Ⓑ   Winners received medals
Ⓒ   Only men took part
Ⓓ   Held in 1896

❹ Objective 4

Which sentence from the article shows the reader that the Olympics are for people around the world?

Ⓐ   *Only men took part.*

Ⓑ   *Each ring stands for a continent.*

Ⓒ   *That's when a Roman emperor ended them.*

Ⓓ   *In 1920 an Olympic flag showed the rings.*

Top 5 Largest Libraries

[1] The largest library in the world is in Washington, D.C. What's the name of this huge collection of books? It is the Library of Congress. It has been gathering books for more than 200 years. Today this library has more than 24 million books. Check out the world's other giant libraries.

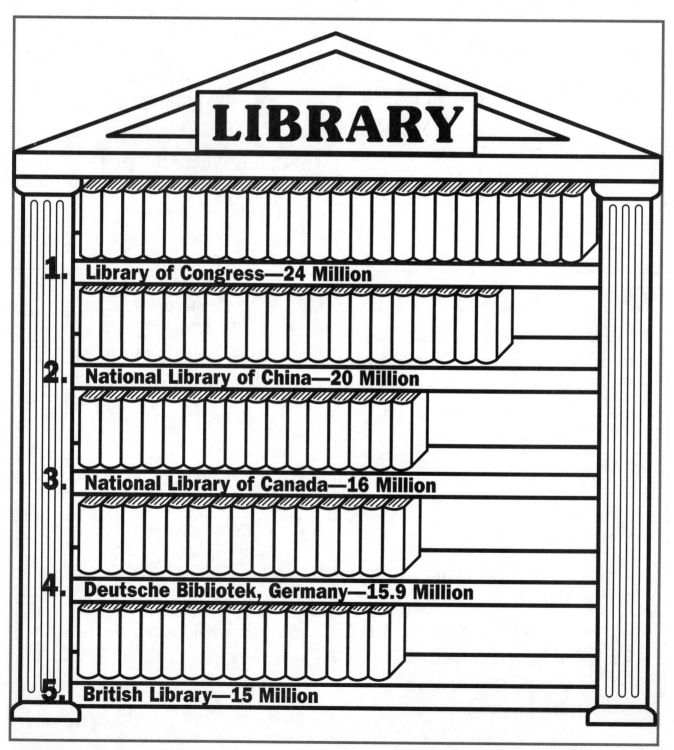

1. Library of Congress—24 Million

2. National Library of China—20 Million

3. National Library of Canada—16 Million

4. Deutsche Bibliotek, Germany—15.9 Million

5. British Library—15 Million

1 Objective 1

This article is mainly about—

(A) the world's best books.

(B) the biggest libraries in the world.

(C) the library in Washington.

(D) the top shelf in a library.

2 Objective 3

This article was written to—

(A) explain how many books are found in the largest libraries.

(B) tell about the books in the library in China.

(C) show the difference between big and small libraries.

(D) tell about the best books in each library.

3 Objective 3

Look at some information from the article.

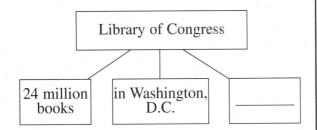

Which idea belongs in the box?

(A) 20 million books
(B) the smallest library
(C) 200 years old
(D) a few books

4 Objective 4

The library with 24 million books is in—

(A) Britain.

(B) China.

(C) Germany.

(D) the United States.

The World's Coral Reefs

1   A coral reef is one of the most beautiful things you can see underwater. Coral looks like rock. But it is really made of living animals. Millions of these very small animals stick together in colonies. They form a hard shell that feels like stone. When lots of colonies grow together, they form giant reefs. They can be all sorts of colors.

2   Coral reefs are found in warm waters near the equator. There are still many coral reefs in the oceans of the world. But not as many as in the past. The reasons? Pollution and global warming are harming these living things.

3   Look at the map below. The red-orange areas on this map are coral reefs.

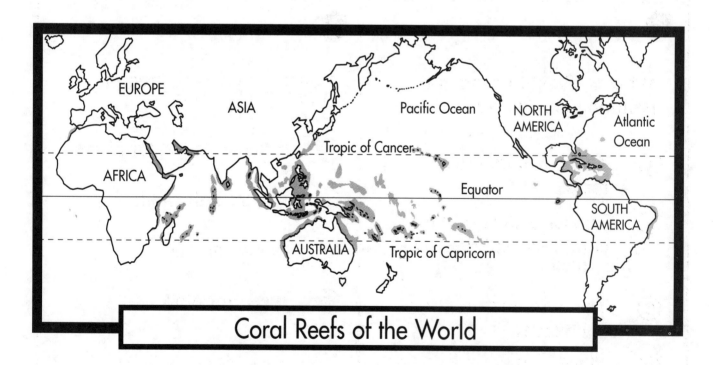

Coral Reefs of the World

❶ Objective 1

In paragraph 1, the word <u>colony</u> means—

Ⓐ different colors.

Ⓑ beautiful things.

Ⓒ a hard shell.

Ⓓ a group of animals.

❷ Objective 2

Why are coral reefs found close to the equator?

Ⓐ The northern waters are polluted

Ⓑ They live in warm waters.

Ⓒ There are many stones near the equator.

Ⓓ They stay together in colonies.

❸ Objective 3

What is likely to happen if pollution gets worse?

Ⓐ There will be fewer reefs.

Ⓑ The hard shell on the coral reef will become soft.

Ⓒ The coral reef will look like leaves.

Ⓓ There will be more coral reefs.

❹ Objective 4

Which statement is true of coral?

Ⓐ It lies in the water alone.

Ⓑ It has a soft shell.

Ⓒ It is an animal.

Ⓓ It is one color.

Fantasy on Ice

Around the World, Artists Make Magic Out of Snow and Ice

By William Pickstand

1   Mix snow, ice, and cold with a big shovelful of imagination. What do you get? You get lots of frozen sculptures!

An Ice Time!

2   Ice sculptures are usually made with chainsaws. A person uses the saw to carve a block of ice into animals, people, or buildings. Every winter you can find ice sculptures in some of the world's coldest cities. The Ice Lantern Festival in Harbin, China, welcomes a million visitors each year. The ice sculptures there are amazing. People looking at them almost forget it is minus 20° Fahrenheit outside!

Snow Joke

3   Ice carving is a very old Chinese custom. But people from all around the world enjoy it.

Ice Carving is amazing. Using tools, statues are created from ice.

1 **Objective 1**

In the title and subtitle, which words help the reader know what <u>Fantasy</u> means?

(A) *out of snow*

(B) *make magic*

(C) *artists make*

(D) *the world*

2 **Objective 1**

Look at these pictures of tools.

1   2   3   4

Which picture is most like the tool in paragraph 2?

(A) Picture 1

(B) Picture 2

(C) Picture 3

(D) Picture 4

3 **Objective 3**

Which is a caption in this article?

(A) *Fantasy on Ice*

(B) *Around the World, Artists Make Magic Out of Snow and Ice*

(C) *An Ice Time!*

(D) *Ice Carving is amazing. Using tools, statues are created from ice.*

4 **Objective 4**

Which statement is true of most of the cities where you can find ice sculptures?

(A) They have a problem.

(B) They have many artists.

(C) They are cold.

(D) They are in the U.S.

Unit 8: CHOOSING OUR LEADERS
Chapter 2: How We Vote

1   In every election thousands of people vote. The U.S. **Constitution** lets each state choose how people should vote. One city may use machines to vote. Another city may use card **ballots**. The most popular way to vote is with punch cards. But sometimes the punch marks are hard to read.

Other Types of Voting

2   Other ways of voting are also popular. One type is a **lever** machine. People press a lever next to the name of a **candidate**. The machine records the candidate's name. Another way to vote is to use handwritten ballots.

What the Future Holds

3   How will people vote in the future? Someday we may vote over the telephone or maybe on the Internet. We might even vote on computer touch screens in special booths. You could just press the screen over the name of the person you want to vote for. Actually, some places are already using machines like these. But they can cost $5,000 each. Not every place can afford them.

Glossary/Definitions

Constitution: the document that gives the basic laws of the United States

ballots: the papers people use to make a secret vote

lever: a bar that you push down to make a machine work

candidate: a person who runs for government office

---

① **Objective 1**

Read the first sentence of the summary below.

> Summary of "How We Vote"
> People in the U.S have voted in different ways.
> _____
> _____

Which of the following completes the summary?

(A) Each state decides how to vote. In the future, we might be using machines to vote.

(B) The most popular way to vote got Florida in trouble. They couldn't decide if Bush or Gore had won.

(C) Older people like handwritten ballots. Younger people prefer machines.

(D) Some people don't vote. Everyone should vote.

② **Objective 2**

What is the main problem with computer touch screens?

(A) They are not correct.

(B) People pick more than one person.

(C) They cost too much.

(D) People are scared of computers.

③ **Objective 3**

Read this outline of information from the article.

> A. How We Vote
>   1. Card ballots
>   2. Punch cards
>   3. _____
>   4. Handwritten ballots

Which information belongs in the blank?

(A) City

(B) Lever

(C) Special

(D) Future

④ **Objective 4**

The author organizes paragraph 3 of the article by—

(A) explaining why it is best to use the lever.

(B) comparing how people in one state vote.

(C) showing a voter using the Internet.

(D) describing ways people might vote in the future.

TIME TO CELEBRATE!

1   When is the New Year celebrated in China? If you said January 1st, you would be wrong. The Chinese New Year takes place between January 21 and February 19. In China, each year is named after an animal. For example, 2002 is the year of the horse.

2   There are 12 animals in all. Every 12 years, the animals are repeated in the same order. Also, each animal has a different trait. Some people believe that if you're born in the year of a certain animal, you will have its trait. For example, people born in the year of the horse will be cheerful.

3   This chart shows the 12 animals and their traits. It also shows what years—past and future—each animal is connected to.

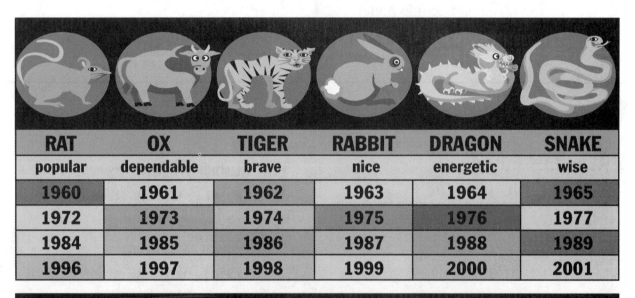

RAT	OX	TIGER	RABBIT	DRAGON	SNAKE
popular	dependable	brave	nice	energetic	wise
1960	1961	1962	1963	1964	1965
1972	1973	1974	1975	1976	1977
1984	1985	1986	1987	1988	1989
1996	1997	1998	1999	2000	2001

HORSE	GOAT	MONKEY	ROOSTER	DOG	PIG
cheerful	artistic	smart	hard working	loyal	good student
1966	1967	1968	1969	1970	1971
1978	1979	1980	1981	1982	1983
1990	1991	1992	1993	1994	1995
2002	2003	2004	2005	2006	2007

1 **Objective 1**

Which animal represents
1995?

Ⓐ rat

Ⓑ dog

Ⓒ pig

Ⓓ snake

2 **Objective 2**

Which of these best describes
a person born in the year of
the tiger?

Ⓐ fearful

Ⓑ popular

Ⓒ nice

Ⓓ fearless

3 **Objective 3**

Children who will be born in
2008 will be under the sign of
the—

Ⓐ pig.

Ⓑ rat.

Ⓒ dog.

Ⓓ ox.

4 **Objective 4**

Which statement is true of
most of the traits in the
Chinese chart?

Ⓐ They are good.

Ⓑ They are alike.

Ⓒ They are bad.

Ⓓ They will repeat every
10 years.

THE STAR-SPANGLED BANNER

1   "The Star-Spangled Banner" is the national anthem of the United States. It was written by Francis Scott Key in 1814. At the time the U.S. and England were at war. Key was an American taken prisoner by the English. He watched the English bomb Fort McHenry, Maryland. They shelled the Americans all night long.

2   In the morning the U.S. flag was still waving. The Americans had not given up. Key was so proud of the U.S. soldiers that he wrote a poem about the battle. Later, the poem was put to music and titled "The Star-Spangled Banner." In 1931 the U.S. Congress made it our nation's anthem.

Oh! say, can you see, by the dawn's early light,

What so proudly we hailed at the twilight's last gleaming?

Whose broad stripes and bright stars, through the perilous fight,

O'er the ramparts we watched, were so gallantly streaming?

And the rockets red glare, the bombs bursting in air,

Gave proof through the night that our flag was still there.

Oh! say, does that Star-Spangled Banner yet wave

O'er the land of the free and the home of the brave?

❶ Objective 1

In paragraph 2, the word <u>anthem</u> means—

Ⓐ song.

Ⓑ heart.

Ⓒ capital.

Ⓓ story.

❷ Objective 2

Why is it important that Francis Scott Key saw the U.S. flag after the bombing?

Ⓐ He was afraid that the Americans would have to sew a new flag.

Ⓑ He was glad that the flag was still flying so that he could be rescued.

Ⓒ He wanted the U.S. Congress to fly that flag in their first meeting.

Ⓓ He felt proud that the Americans had not given up and wrote a poem about it.

❸ Objective 3

Read the chart below. It shows the order in which some events happened in the article.

England and U.S. were at war.
↓
_____
↓
Key watched the bombing of Fort McHenry.
↓
The U.S. flag was still waving.

Which of these belongs in the empty box?

Ⓐ The poem was put to music.

Ⓑ Key wrote a poem.

Ⓒ Key became a prisoner.

Ⓓ The poem became the national anthem.

❹ Objective 4

Which words from the national anthem show what Key saw at night?

Ⓐ *that our flag was still there*

Ⓑ *the bombs bursting in air*

Ⓒ *land of the free*

Ⓓ *dawn's early light*

© *Teacher Created Materials, Inc.*   63   *#8652 TAKS Nonfiction Reading—Level 2*

PEOPLE AROUND THE WORLD
The Indians of Brazil

1   Hundreds of years ago, people from Europe first visited Brazil, a nation in South America. In those days about 30 million Indians lived in Brazil. There were hundreds of native tribes. Today, there are only about 300,000 Indians left in Brazil.

Disappearing Indians

2   There are many reasons that the Indians disappeared. The first Europeans made slaves of the Indians. The Europeans also brought new sicknesses. The Indians were not used to the germs, and many died.

The Problem Continues

3   Today, Brazil has no slavery. But many Indian tribes are still in danger. One of these tribes is called the Yonomami. They are dying of malaria. This sickness is brought in by workers from the outside world. The workers are looking for gold in the Amazon rain forest. The government of Brazil has promised to protect the Yonomami. But the government has not been able to keep that promise. The future doesn't look good for the rain forest tribes.

Words From the Rain Forest

Indians of Brazil have their own languages. Sometimes words from these tribes become part of the English language. Here are a few familiar Indian words and what they mean.

1. tobacco (toe-back-oh): a plant with leaves that can be smoked or chewed

2. hammock (ha-muck): a bed made of netting. It hangs above the ground.

3. tapioca (ta-pea-oh-kuh): pudding made from the roots of a plant

4. jaguar (jag-wahr): a big cat found in Central and South America

1

Objective 1

The article is mainly about—

(A) the plants of the rain forest.

(B) the Yonomani tribe.

(C) how the tribes of Brazil are dying.

(D) the tobacco fields.

2

Objective 3

Look at the information from the article.

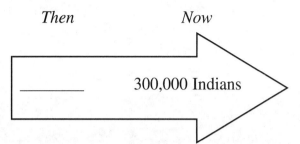

Then   *Now*

_____ 300,000 Indians

Which of these goes in the blank?

(A) 30 Indians

(B) 30,000 Indians

(C) 3,000,000 Indians

(D) 30,000,000 Indians

3

Objective 3

Look at the drawing of information from the article.

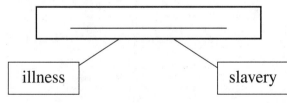

illness   slavery

What goes in the box?

(A) Why look for gold?

(B) Why are Indians disappearing?

(C) What will happen in the future?

(D) What grows in the rain forest?

4

Objective 4

The author organizes this article by—

(A) telling about the problems of tribes and telling about their language.

(B) showing how to save the tribes.

(C) showing Indians dying of illness.

(D) telling the differences between the tribes of South America.

Web Page

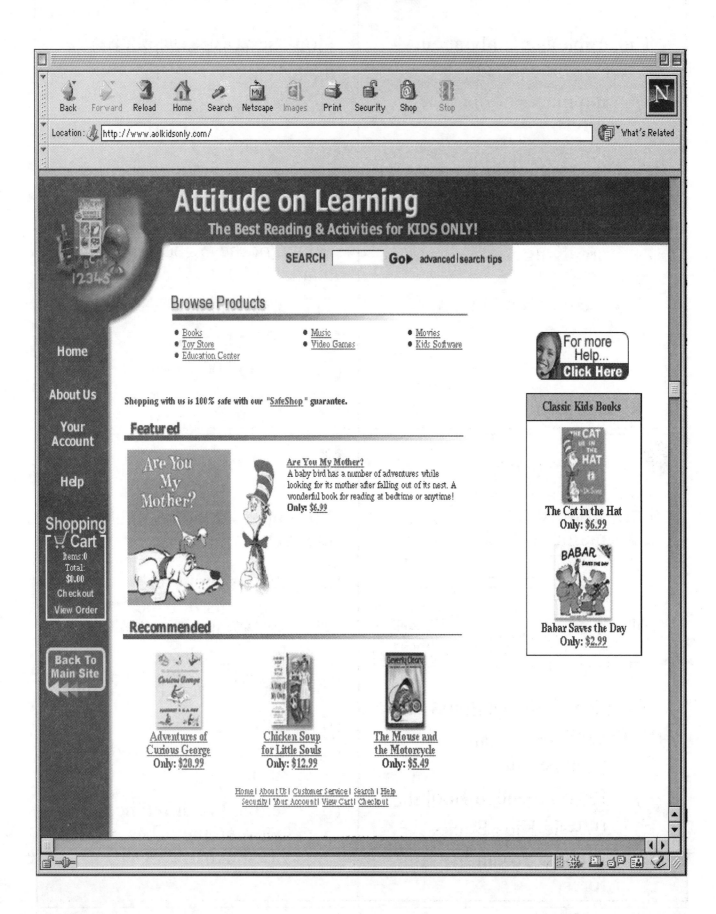

Attitude on Learning
The Best Reading & Activities for KIDS ONLY!

SEARCH [   ] Go▶ advanced | search tips

Browse Products

- Books
- Toy Store
- Education Center
- Music
- Video Games
- Movies
- Kids Software

Shopping with us is 100% safe with our "SafeShop" guarantee.

Featured

Are You My Mother?
A baby bird has a number of adventures while looking for its mother after falling out of its nest. A wonderful book for reading at bedtime or anytime!
Only: $6.99

Recommended

Adventures of Curious George
Only: $20.99

Chicken Soup for Little Souls
Only: $12.99

The Mouse and the Motorcycle
Only: $5.49

Home | About US | Customer Service | Search | Help
Security | Your Account | View Cart | Checkout

Home

About Us

Your Account

Help

Shopping Cart
Items:0
Total:
$0.00
Checkout
View Order

Back To Main Site

For more Help... Click Here

Classic Kids Books

The Cat in the Hat
Only: $6.99

Babar Saves the Day
Only: $2.99

Location: http://www.aolkidsonly.com/   What's Related

Back Forward Reload Home Search Netscape Images Print Security Shop Stop

❶ Objective 1

The Web page is mainly about—

- Ⓐ children's books.
- Ⓑ reading.
- Ⓒ shopping.
- Ⓓ kids only.

❷ Objective 2

How much does the book, "Are You My Mother?" cost?

- Ⓐ $6.99
- Ⓑ $20.99
- Ⓒ $12.99
- Ⓓ $5.49

❸ Objective 3

Look at the diagram of information from the article.

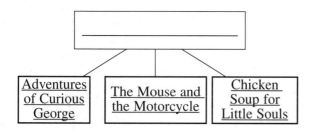

What idea belongs in the empty box?

- Ⓐ Featured Books
- Ⓑ Recommended Books
- Ⓒ Classic Kids Books
- Ⓓ Browse Products

❹ Objective 4

Who would most likely use the Web site?

- Ⓐ moms and dads
- Ⓑ authors and illustrators
- Ⓒ grandmas and grandpas
- Ⓓ kids and teachers

Dear Aunt Mary and Uncle George,

Thank you very much for my birthday gift. I really like the watch you gave me. Thanks for the extra battery, too. If my watch stops, I can put in the new battery. I also like the cartoon character on the face of the watch. All my friends think it's cool.

I also want to thank you for the money you gave me. I didn't see it right away. Not until I opened my birthday card. I will put the money in the bank. One day I will use it for college.

The lunch you took me to was also great. It was the nicest restaurant I ever ate in. I liked the fancy cheeseburger. But the best part was the dessert. The chocolate cake was great. So was the whipped cream on it. The ice cream soda was good, too.

Thank you again. You are the best aunt and uncle in the world. I love you both. I can't wait until my next birthday!

Your nephew,

Derek

1 **Objective 1**

This article is mainly about—

(A) a birthday party for a young boy.

(B) a birthday lunch for a boy at a nice restaurant.

(C) a boy thanking his aunt and uncle for birthday gifts.

(D) a boy's new birthday watch from his aunt and uncle.

2 **Objective 2**

The boy likes his birthday lunch because—

(A) he saw a cartoon character at the restaurant.

(B) he had never eaten in a restaurant before.

(C) he got to take a friend with him to the restaurant for his birthday lunch.

(D) it was the best restaurant he had ever been to.

3 **Objective 3**

What happened after Derek ate his cheeseburger?

(A) He had chocolate cake for dessert.

(B) He put the battery in his watch.

(C) He opened his birthday card.

(D) He went to eat at a nice restaurant.

4 **Objective 4**

What can the reader tell about Derek from reading this article?

(A) He knows how to tell time.

(B) He likes to spend time with his aunt and uncle.

(C) He likes to watch cartoons on the T.V.

(D) His favorite kind of cake is chocolate cake.

By George, It's a Brand New Book!

A Curious Story

By Laura C. Girardi

1   Curious George is a very famous book character. The monkey was created by Hans Augusto Rey and his wife, Margret. They also came up with a character named Whiteblack the Penguin. No one has heard of Whiteblack.

2   Hans and Margret wrote about Whiteblack 63 years ago. After they wrote the tale, it got lost. The two writers are no longer alive. But Whiteblack is! The story Hans and Margret wrote a long time ago is finally in bookstores. The title of the book is *Whiteblack the Penguin Sees the World*.

An Amazing Penguin

3   Whiteblack lives in Penguinland. He wants to take a trip to see new things. That way Whiteblack can tell stories about his travels on his radio show. On his trip Whiteblack sees his first human. Whiteblack says, "Why, he looks just like me! White shirt, dark coat, and he walks on two legs."

Whiteblack Meets the World

4   The story of Whiteblack was never printed. How did it finally become a book? Readers can thank Anita Silvey. Silvey had seen pictures of Whiteblack hanging up at a show. She thought the pictures were great. Silvey works for a company that makes books. She got her company to print the story. Silvey said, "It's as if I found one of the Reys' children who had been in an orphanage."

1 Objective 1

According to the article, why does Whiteblack take a trip in the book?

(A) He wants to visit Curious George.

(B) He is just learning how to walk.

(C) He wanted to go to Penguinland.

(D) He wants to see new things.

2 Objective 2

What is the main problem in the article?

(A) The story about Whiteblack was written a very long time ago.

(B) The story about Whiteblack got lost.

(C) People didn't like the name Whiteblack.

(D) Hans and Margaret Rey are no longer alive.

3 Objective 3

Read the chart below. It shows the order in which some events happened in the article.

Hans and Margaret Rey wrote a story about Whiteblack.
↓
The story about Whiteblack got lost.
↓
↓
Silvey worked with her company to get them to print the story.

Which of these belongs in the empty box?

(A) The book was written 63 years ago.

(B) Hans and Margaret Rey wrote stories about Curious George.

(C) Anita Silvey saw pictures of Whiteblack at an art show.

(D) The title of the book was "Whiteblack the Penguin Sees the World."

4 Objective 4

What can the reader tell about the writer, Anita Silvey?

(A) She was excited to find the pictures of Whiteblack.

(B) She always wanted to write a story about a penguin.

(C) Her favorite pictures are in black and white.

(D) This is the first book that she has ever written.

Who Turned Off the Lights?

By Nellie Gonzalez Cutler

1   (SACRAMENTO, California, January 19) California has a power problem. The state can't make enough electricity for everyone. The state government wants everyone to use as little power as possible. They have asked people in California to use less electricity. Some businesses work with fewer lights during the day. Not long ago, things got even worse. A big storm hit California. That made it harder for the power companies to produce electricity.

Companies With a Problem

2   Two big companies produce almost all the state's power. The companies serve 25 million customers. The companies are spending a lot of money to bring electricity to the people of California. But they have a big problem. The companies keep spending more and more to produce electricity. But the companies are not allowed to charge their customers more money. So the companies are not able to make enough power.

3   People in the state government hope they can solve the power problem. Gray Davis is the governor of California. He isn't worried. He thinks the future of power in California is bright. Davis says: "We can see the light at the end of the tunnel."

❶ Objective 1

Read the meanings below for the word <u>power</u>.

> **power** (pou´er) noun
>
> **1.** the force to do something **2.** being able to control others **3.** a person or group that has control over others **4.** energy that can be used for doing work

Which meaning best fits the way <u>power</u> is used in paragraph 1?

- Ⓐ Meaning 1
- Ⓑ Meaning 2
- Ⓒ Meaning 3
- Ⓓ Meaning 4

❷ Objective 2

What is the main problem in the article?

- Ⓐ People leave their lights on too long.
- Ⓑ The state does not have enough electricity.
- Ⓒ A big storm hit the state of California.
- Ⓓ Many shoppers have to shop in the dark.

❸ Objective 3

Look at the diagram of information from the article.

```
        Why the companies can't
        make enough power?
         /                \
The companies serve    The companies spend
25 million people.     a lot of money.
               |
        [                ]
```

Which idea belongs in the empty box?

- Ⓐ There is a power problem.
- Ⓑ The companies can't make the people pay more money.
- Ⓒ The workers leave the lights on too long.
- Ⓓ Stores use too much power.

❹ Objective 4

What will the governor probably do in the future?

- Ⓐ Help with the power problem.
- Ⓑ Turn his lights off.
- Ⓒ Put a light at the end of a tunnel.
- Ⓓ Worry about the power.

A Diary From Long Ago

April 16, 1775

1   I do not have much time to write today. First, I had to bring in the vegetables from the garden. Next, I sewed together my new dress. Then I helped Ma cook dinner. Pa and brother Charlie were out in the fields. Ma is worried. She says there are lots of English soldiers in nearby towns. There are also lots of patriots around. Ma says something bad is going to happen. The patriots want to have a battle with the English Redcoats. Charlie wants to fight for the patriots.   Charlie is only ten—a year older than I am. He must turn 16 before he can be a soldier. Charlie does not care.

April 17, 1775

2   Between chores Ma let me read today. She says girls don't need book learning. But I like reading and writing. Maybe one day I can go to school.

3   Later, I made buttons for my dress. I used some animal bones. I also stuffed goose feathers into my pillow. Now it is nice and soft.

April 18, 1775

4   Everyone thinks the English and Americans will fight soon. I stayed up late waiting for news of war. I finally fell asleep. But late at night, someone was yelling and woke me up. I heard a horseman ride by very fast. He was screaming, "The British are coming!" Charlie said the man was Paul Revere. Charlie grabbed a gun he uses to hunt turkeys. He wants to fight the British. But Pa took the gun away. He said Charlie is too young. He told Charlie to leave the fighting to grown ups.

5   Ma is right. Something is about to happen. When it does, I hope our family gets through it okay.

1 Objective 1

How old is the girl who wrote this diary?

(A) 9

(B) 10

(C) 16

(D) 17

2 Objective 2

What is the main problem in the story?

(A) A man is yelling and wakes the girl up.

(B) Pa took Charlie's gun away.

(C) A war is starting between the English and the Americans.

(D) There are too many chores for a young girl to do.

3 Objective 3

Look at the diagram of information from the article.

What idea belongs in the empty box?

(A) Chores the girl does on April 16

(B) Chores the girl does on April 17

(C) Chores the girl does on April 18

(D) Chores the girl does with Charlie

4 Objective 4

Which sentence best shows that the girl would like to learn?

(A) *Ma is right.*

(B) *Maybe one day I can go to school.*

(C) *Charlie does not care.*

(D) *Later, I made buttons for my dress.*

Up, Up, and Away!

Two Young Pilots Fly Around the World

By Kathryn Hoffman

1   Dan Dominguez and Chris Wall had a dream. They wanted to be the youngest pilots to fly around the world. Dan and Chris both grew up in El Paso, Texas and are both 22 years old. A few years ago they learned how to fly planes. Soon after, they had an idea: to fly around the world together. A few years later they bought a small plane. Companies gave Chris and Dan money to help them take their trip. Their plan was about to take off!

Around the World

2   Dan and Chris flew over five continents. What was the best part of their trip? Sharing it with kids. Many classes followed their flight on the Internet. "We got e-mails every day," says Wall.

3   The pilots visited 18 countries. Their favorite stop was in India. That's because they talked to 1,000 students there.

Telling Their Story

4   Dan and Chris became the youngest pilots to circle the Earth. But their trip isn't over. They want to tell their story to schools around the country. They want kids to know that dreams come true—with hard work.

Legends of the Air

In 1927, at age 25, Charles Lindbergh flew from New York to Paris, France. He was the first to do this nonstop and alone.

In 1936, Beryl Markham became the first person to fly alone across the Atlantic from east to west. She was 34 years old.

Chuck Yeager broke the sound barrier at age 24 on Oct. 14, 1947. He was the first person to travel more than 600 miles an hour!

1

Objective 1

Read the first sentence of the summary below.

Summary of "Up, Up, and Away!"
Two young men had a dream to fly around the
world together.

_____

_____

Which of the following completes the summary above?

- (A) They are both 22 years old and grew up in El Paso, Texas.
- (B) Their dreams came true when they bought their own plane and became the youngest pilots to circle the earth.
- (C) They got e-mails from students every day and now they want kids to know that dreams can come true.
- (D) They learned how to fly planes and then a few years later, they bought a small plane.

2

Objective 1

According to the last section of the article, how old was Chuck Yeager when he broke the sound barrier?

- (A) 14
- (B) 24
- (C) 34
- (D) 47

3

Objective 3

Read the chart below. It shows the order in which some events happened in the

---
| Dan and Charlie learned how to fly. |

| They bought their own small airplane. |

| |

| They became the youngest pilots to circle the Earth. |

Which of these belongs in the empty box?

- (A) They visited 18 countries.
- (B) They dreamed of being the youngest pilots to fly around the world.
- (C) They grew up in El Paso, Texas.
- (D) They want kids to follow their dreams.

4

Objective 4

What will Dan and Chris probably do in the future?

- (A) send e-mails to the kids who sent them e-mails
- (B) have a new dream to start working on
- (C) fly around the world again
- (D) visit schools and talk to students

The Daily Squawker

A Short Summer Means a Smarter Student

1   Everyone loves summer vacation. Especially kids. They've worked hard all year. Their reward is to get two months off. But is this a good thing? We think the answer is: No! Our children need to stay in school longer each year. That way they can learn much more. A shorter vacation would lead to higher test scores. Kids would get a better education.

The Plan

2   We believe the school year should be five weeks longer. Students would get a three-week summer vacation. That is still a lot of time. Critics may say: Schools will be hot in the summer. What if they do not have air conditioners? We say: Use electric fans!

More Good Reasons

3   A longer school year means smarter students. But it also means happier parents. Many parents like it when their kids are in school. They worry when their children have too much free time. Parents feel their children are safe in school.

4   Some parents send their kids to camp all summer. That can cost a lot. With our plan summer camp would be no longer than three weeks. It would cost much less.

5   There is one bad part to this plan: Teachers will have to work longer. But maybe they could be paid more.

6   Summer is a great time—to stay in school.

❶ Objective 1

This article is mainly about—

(A) schools being very hot in the summer.

(B) students staying in school longer during a school year.

(C) students like their summers away from school.

(D) students making better test scores in the summer months.

❷ Objective 3

The most likely reason the author wrote this article was to—

(A) persuade readers that school should be held five weeks longer each year.

(B) tell readers about a school where students go to school all but three weeks of the year.

(C) explain what students will do if they go to school longer in the year.

(D) comparing test scores of boys to those of girls.

❸ Objective 3

Read the diagram of information from the article.

Which idea belongs in the empty circle?

(A) Students will use the school's air conditioning.

(B) Students work hard during the school year.

(C) Students could have summer camp at school in the summer.

(D) Students would get higher test scores.

❹ Objective 4

Which sentence in the article best shows that the parents think it is important for kids to keep busy?

(A) *That is still a lot of time.*

(B) *Students would get a three-week summer vacation.*

(C) *They worry when their children have too much free time.*

(D) *Some parents send their kids to camp all summer.*

Search: Pets

Previous   Next

Best Sites

1. Pets: Everything about how to care for your pet.
2. Pet Talk: You can talk about your pet and hear about others' pets.
3. Pet Time: Shop for all kinds of pet supplies.

Sites That Match

1. PetShop.com—order supplies online for your cat, dog, birds, lizards, spiders, ferrets, fish, snakes or any other pet.

www.pet_shop.com

2. Pet Gerbils—lots of fun facts about this amazing little rodent. Photos and information on nature's cutest critter! For beginners and long-time owners.

www.pet1gerbil.com

3. My Two Pets—see photos of my two dogs, Billy and Red. They are bulldogs. Read all about them. I love them very much. And you will see why.

www.mytwopets.com

4. Pet Care, Inc.—nationwide chain of animal hospitals. We will treat your pet for any illness. Full-time ainmal doctors on staff. See Web site for office hours, directions, prices.

www.petcareinc.com

5. Pet Shop Boys—official fan club of the best band ever! This singing group from England is tops. Photos and bulletin board. Pet Shop Boys rule!

www.pet_shopboys.com

6. Smart Doggy—take this quiz and find out your dog's I.Q. Takes only 15 minutes. You'll finally know for sure if your pooch is a brainiac or a dumb-dumb.

www.smartdoggy.org

7. Pet Painter—I will draw your dog, cat, parakeet, or whatever pet you own. I can put the owner in the picture. Pet portraits make great gifts.

www.petpainter.com

8. P.E.T. Car Service—air-conditioned cars go anywhere around town. Comfortable and cheap. Check out special rates for businesses.

www.petcarservice.com

1–8 of 61,086

1   **Objective 1**

What word did the person enter to make a search?

(A)   Pets

(B)   Pet talk

(C)   Pet Time

(D)   *PetShop.com*

2   **Objective 1**

Which two sites do not have anything to do with pets?

(A)   Pet Painter and Pet Shop Boys

(B)   Pet Shop Boys and P.E.T. Car Service

(C)   P.E.T. Car Service and Smart Doggy

(D)   My Two Pets and Pet Painter

3   **Objective 3**

Look at the diagram of information from the article.

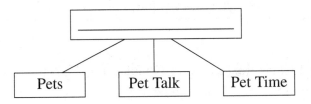

Which idea belongs in the empty box?

(A)   Pet Care Sites

(B)   Sites That Match

(C)   Best Sites

(D)   Search Sites

4   **Objective 4**

What can the reader tell about the person who did this search?

(A)   The person is a girl.

(B)   The person's parents said no to a pet.

(C)   The person wants to talk to other people about a pet.

(D)   The person is interested in information about pets.

A Busy New President

By Kathryn Hoffman

1   George W. Bush works fast. On January 20 he was sworn in as president. That same day, workers were busy at the White House. They were making changes to the Oval Office—the president's office. It was being painted a different color. Workers also put down new rugs. Bush even added a new rule: People should not wear jeans in the White House.

Big Plans for Schools

2   Those aren't the only changes Bush is making. The new president has big plans. And he wants those plans to start right away. In his first 180 days Bush hopes to improve America's schools and cut taxes. He has already told Congress about his education plan. His goal is to make schools better. He would like local people to have more control of their own schools. He wants kids to take a lot more tests in math and English.

3   President Bush wanted to show he was serious about education. So he visited an elementary school in Washington, D.C. He told students, "It's a real treat to be able to look children in the eye and wish them all the best."

Some White House Facts

- There are 132 rooms and 32 bathrooms in the White House. There are also 412 doors, 147 windows, 28 fireplaces, 7 staircases, and 3 elevators.

- About 6,000 people visit the White House each day.

- It takes 570 gallons of paint to cover the outside of the White House.

- The White House has a tennis court, a jogging track, a swimming pool, a movie theater, and a bowling lane.

---

① **Objective 1**

The second paragraph is mainly about—

(A) the changes Bush made in his office.

(B) how Bush hopes to make America's schools better.

(C) Bush visiting schools in Washington D.C.

(D) Bush and his wife dancing at a party.

② **Objective 2**

According to the article, how many people visit the White House each day?

(A) 412

(B) 147

(C) 6000

(D) 570

③ **Objective 3**

Look at the web about changes that Bush made in the White House.

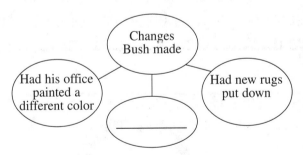

Which idea belongs in the empty oval?

(A) Made a rule that people should not wear jeans

(B) Made a rule to stop dancing

(C) Changed his office from square to oval

(D) Made changes in the schools

④ **Objective 4**

The author organizes the last section of this article by—

(A) telling stories about the White House.

(B) writing math problems about the White House.

(C) listing facts about the White House.

(D) giving readers information about George W. Bush.

Walt Disney

1   Walt Disney was one of the greatest cartoon makers in history. His work is loved by both kids and adults.

2   Disney was born in Chicago, Illionois, in 1901. When he was young, he liked to draw cartoons. He even studied cartooning in school. His first job was as an illustrator in Kansas City. After a while, he started to make animated cartoons. These are cartoons that move.

A Mouse Named Mickey

3   Eventually, Disney moved to Los Angeles, California. There, in 1927, he came up with a cartoon character. The character was a little rodent called Mickey Mouse. In 1928, Mickey starred in a short cartoon called "Steamboat Willie." This was one of the first animated cartoons with sound. Disney invented more characters, such as Donald Duck, Pluto, and Goofy.

4   In the 1930's, Disney began to make longer animated cartoons. The first was Snow White and the Seven Dwarfs. Other popular ones were Pinocchio, Dumbo, and Fantasia. Disney also made movies with real people. His first was The Absent-Minded Professor.

5   Walt Disney's next great idea was to build an amusement park. In 1955, Disneyland opened. People visited it from all over the world. So Disney decided to build another amusement park in Orlando, Florida. In 1966, work began. But in that same year Walt Disney died. He never lived to see his second park open.

Important Dates

1901: born in Chicago, Illinois

1927: invents the cartoon character Mickey Mouse

1935: produces his first full-length feature cartoon, *Snow White and the Seven Dwarfs*

1940: opens his cartoon studio in Burbank, California

1955: opens Disneyland in Anaheim, California

1961: produces his first real-life movie, *The Absent-Minded Professor*

1966: Disney dies

❶ **Objective 1**

Which of the following is the best summary of the article?

Ⓐ Walt Disney was a great cartoon maker. He created Mickey Mouse, Donald Duck and other popular characters. People from all over the world visit Disney's famous park, Disneyland.

Ⓑ Walt Disney grew up in Chicago. Then he moved to California.

Ⓒ Walt Disney loved to draw cartoons. He studied cartoon making at school. When he moved to California he came up with his Mickey Mouse character.

Ⓓ Walt Disney is known for making Mickey Mouse. He first came up with Mickey in 1927. Then in 1928, he made a cartoon movie with his new character.

❷ **Objective 1**

According to the article, what year did Disney begin work in his new park in Florida?

Ⓐ 1930

Ⓑ 1940

Ⓒ 1955

Ⓓ 1966

❸ **Objective 3**

This article was written mainly to—

Ⓐ explain how cartoons are made.

Ⓑ compare cartoons to real movie characters.

Ⓒ tell readers about a famous cartoon maker.

Ⓓ tell a story about Mickey Mouse.

❹ **Objective 4**

What can you tell about Walt Disney from reading the article?

Ⓐ He really liked animals and that is why he liked to draw animals in his cartoons.

Ⓑ Even at a young age, he knew what he wanted to do with his life.

Ⓒ He thought that cartoon movies were better than movies with real people.

Ⓓ He did not like living in Chicago and that is why he built a park in Florida.

SUMMER OF THE SHARK

Shark Attacks on the Rise

By Bill Doyle

1   (Miami, Florida, September 14) Sharks don't really like to bite people. A great white shark would rather eat a seal. A bull shark loves fish and even another shark! Then why has there been scary news about shark attacks? Scientists say that is a good question.

Why Sharks Attack

2   One reason for the high numbers of attacks lately is that more people are in the ocean than ever before. Many splash around in the morning and early evening. That's when sharks hunt.

3   Sharks that attack humans are probably confused. They might mistake a human foot for a fish. "Sharks are not out to get humans," says scientist Dr. Robert Lea. "It is just humans sharing a spot in the ocean with sharks at the wrong time."

Dont' Sweat It

4   Don't be afraid. The odds of being attacked by a shark are very slim.

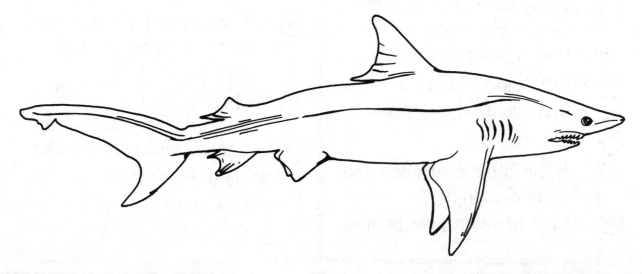

1   Objective 1

According to the article, what is one reason a shark might bite a human?

Ⓐ   They are hungry and want food to eat.

Ⓑ   People scare the fish away that sharks want to eat.

Ⓒ   They might think a person's foot is a fish.

Ⓓ   They don't want people to swim in their ocean.

2   Objective 2

Which of the following best tells how a shark might feel if it attacks a human?

Ⓐ   confused

Ⓑ   mad

Ⓒ   scary

Ⓓ   afraid

3   Objective 3

Look at the diagram of information about sharks.

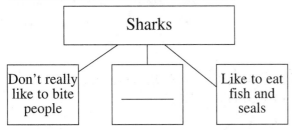

Which idea belongs in the empty box?

Ⓐ   Swim with other sharks
Ⓑ   Are very slim
Ⓒ   Hunt in the mornings and early evenings
Ⓓ   Like to swim near people

4   Objective 4

What can the reader tell about swimming in the ocean from reading this article?

Ⓐ   It might be safer to swim in the morning.

Ⓑ   It might be safer to swim in the evening.

Ⓒ   It is never safe to swim in the ocean.

Ⓓ   It might be safer to swim in the afternoon.

The Daily News

Help the Poor

Dear Editor:

1   I am seeing more and more homeless people on the streets. They beg for money to buy food. They have no place to sleep. In the winter they are cold. In the summer they are hot. Most people don't even look at them. They pretend they're not there.

2   This is a disgrace. I think we must do something to help poor people. If you have extra money, give some to charities. Many charities help feed poor people. Others give them old clothes.

3   We can also give our time. People can spend a few hours a week working for charities. They could work in soup kitchens. Or work in thrift shops that give the money made to charity.

4   But the city must also help. The government must find jobs for poor people. They must also build shelters for them. That way, poor people will have a place to live. Also, more food must be given away to needy people. I have seen homeless families. I felt very sad when I saw the children. These kids were dressed in rags. They could not go to school and learn. They were thin and dirty. This is no way to treat our children!

5   I am giving my time and money to charity. I hope you do, too!

Sincerely,

Joseph Dabble
Chastenville

1 **Objective 1**

Read the meanings below for the word <u>place</u>.

place (plās) *noun*

1. an area; region **2.** a location, as a city **3.** a short city street or a public square **4.** an area; like a building or a home

Which meaning best fits the way <u>place</u> is used in the first paragraph of the article?

(A) Meaning 1

(B) Meaning 2

(C) Meaning 3

(D) Meaning 4

2 **Objective 2**

Which of these best describes how Joseph Dabble feels about the treatment of homeless people?

(A) poor and sleepy

(B) hot and cold

(C) old and needy

(D) upset and sad

3 **Objective 4**

The most likely reason the author wrote this article was to—

(A) give readers facts about homeless people.

(B) persuade readers to help the homeless.

(C) explain to readers how homeless people might look.

(D) tell readers what it is like to be homeless.

4 **Objective 4**

What can the reader tell about Joseph from reading the article?

(A) He cares about other people.

(B) He used to be homeless.

(C) He comes from a poor family.

(D) He has saved a lot of money.

Back Off, Bullies!

How to Stop Getting Picked On

By Elizabeth Siris

1   Christian Champ is 10 years old. But the first time he met a bully was in kindergarten. A second-grader pushed Christian off a swing. Christian is in fifth grade now. He knows how to handle bullies. "First ignore the bully," he says. "Then tell the teacher."

Big, Bad Bully

2   No one likes to be pushed or teased. But this happens to lots of kids every day. A report says that five million kids are bullied each year. About 160,000 kids skip school every day. They do it to keep away from bullies.

Stopping Bullies

3   Many schools are trying to end the problem. These schools have programs about bullies. The programs show kids why bullying is bad. They teach kids not to hit or tease. Bullies often tease because words can hurt.

4   Will these new programs stop teasing and fighting? Bullies can change, says a boy named Spencer. He's a 10-year-old from Colorado. Spencer says, "I teased people when I was in second grade. But by third grade, I stopped. I didn't like making people feel bad."

WHAT SHOULD YOU DO IF A BULLY BOTHERS YOU?

- Tell a parent or a teacher. Parents and teachers want to know what happened and how you feel about it. You are not being a tattletale.
- If the bullying took place at school, have a parent talk to your teacher. Parents should not call the parents of the bully.
- Look the bully in the eye and walk away confidently. Don't fight.
- Bullies want to hurt your feelings. Even if they're being really mean, act as if they're not succeeding.
- Stand up for students who are bullied. Ask them to stand up for you.

---

1   **Objective 1**

According to the article, what is the one way to stop bullying?

(A)   have a program at school about bullies

(B)   have students skip school

(C)   keep students away from bullies

(D)   make the bullies feel bad

2   **Objective 2**

What is the main problem in the article?

(A)   A bully pushed Christian off a swing.

(B)   Millions of children are bullied each year.

(C)   Bullies tease second graders.

(D)   Bullies want you to stay home.

3   **Objective 3**

What does Christian say to do after you ignore the bully?

(A)   ignore the bully

(B)   take a swing at the bully

(C)   tease the bully

(D)   tell the teacher

4   **Objective 4**

The author organizes the last part of the article by—

(A)   telling a story about a bully.

(B)   explaining why bullies act mean to others.

(C)   listing tips for dealing with bullies.

(D)   asking questions about bullies.

Planting Corn

Fresh corn on the cob is tasty! You can buy corn in a store. But it's more fun to grow your own corn. Here's how.

1. Buy sweet corn seeds.

2. Wait until the spring. The ground must be warm from the sun.

3. Dig a row of holes. Each hole should be 1 inch deep. The holes should be about 5 inches apart.

4. You can dig a few rows of holes. The rows should be about 3 feet from each other.

5. Place a seed in each hole. Then cover it over with the dirt.

6. Water the seeds every day.

7. Wait until the corn plants are 1 to $1\frac{1}{2}$ feet tall. Then add fertilizer (FUR-tuh-lie-zer) to the soil. Fertilizer helps the plants grow better.

8. Watch your plant grow for about 75 days. By then, the corn should be ripe. An ear of corn has "silks." These are long yellow strings that hang from the ear. When the silks turn brown, pick the corn.

9. Squash a corn kernel with your thumb. Milky juice should come out. That means the corn is ready to cook.

10. Have an adult cook the corn for a short time. Then eat it. Yum!

❶ Objective 1

In step 7, which words help the reader know what <u>fertilizer</u> means?

(A) *the corn plants*

(B) *to the soil*

(C) *helps the plants grow better*

(D) *1 to 1½ feet tall*

❷ Objective 2

According to the article, why is it important to plant the seeds in spring?

(A) The ground is warm.

(B) Seeds are on sale in the stores.

(C) The ground is easier to dig.

(D) There is more water.

❸ Objective 3

Read the chart below. It shows the order in which some events happened in the article.

| Dig a row of holes in the ground. |
| Put seeds in the holes. |
| _____ |
| Pick the corn. |

Which of these belongs in the empty box?

(A) Get some corn seeds at a store.

(B) Be sure to water the seeds each day.

(C) Taste the corn.

(D) Ask an adult to cook the corn.

❹ Objective 4

The author organizes this article by

(A) listing facts about corn.

(B) explaining how farmers grow crops.

(C) listing steps for growing corn.

(D) telling how to cook corn.

Wearing a Helmet Is Cool.

Not Wearing a Helmet Is Foolish.

Think a bike helmet is for nerds?
Then think about these facts:

- More than 400,000 kids go to the hospital every year because they are hurt riding bikes.

- Five hundred people die every year because they don't wear bike helmets.

- Only one of every seven kids always wears a helmet when biking.

Now think about this fact:
Wearing a helmet cuts the chance of injuring your head by 85%.

Riding a bike, a scooter, or skates without a helmet is dangerous. You can get a serious head injury. Always wear a helmet. And follow these simple rules:

Make sure your helmet fits well.
Buckle your chinstrap.
Don't forget to wear elbow and knee pads.

Remember: A helmet could save your life.

This ad is brought to you by the United States Council of Safety.

① **Objective 1**

This article is mainly about—

Ⓐ kids who go to the hospital each year because they get hurt on bikes.

Ⓑ kids who think that wearing a bike helmet is a cool thing to do.

Ⓒ wearing a helmet when riding bikes, scooters, and skates.

Ⓓ wearing bike helmets and how they keep kids safe from injuries.

② **Objective 1**

Why is it important to wear a helmet?

Ⓐ It looks cool.

Ⓑ It protects your head.

Ⓒ It keeps your head warm.

Ⓓ It is foolish not to wear one.

③ **Objective 3**

This article was written mainly to—

Ⓐ give facts about bike helmets and safety.

Ⓑ show kids what cool helmets look like.

Ⓒ tell a story about kids who didn't wear helmets.

Ⓓ explain how to put a helmet on.

④ **Objective 4**

What can the reader tell about the Council of Safety?

Ⓐ They go to hospitals a lot to see kids who got hurt on bikes and were not wearing helmets.

Ⓑ They think it is important for kids to know about bike helmets.

Ⓒ They don't like kids to ride bikes.

Ⓓ They like to write a lot of rules for kids.

Top 5 Ice Cream Flavors

1   The first ice cream was served to the Roman emperor Nero in 62 A.D. This was nearly 2,000 years before the first Ben and Jerry's opened. The Roman treat was made of snow, nectar, fruit, and honey. Here's the scoop on the best-selling flavors in the U.S. today.

Best-Selling Flavors

Gallons a year Sold (in millions)

| Vanilla (171) | Chocolate (57) | Neapolitan (47) | Butter pecan (25) | Cookies and cream (20) |

Your Turn

Use the graph to answer these questions.

1. What's the fifth-most popular flavor?

2. How many gallons of chocolate were sold?

3. Find the number of gallons of vanilla sold. Is it more than or less than the number of gallons of the other four flavors combined?

4. What is the second-most popular flavor?

1 Objective 1

According to the article ice cream was first served in—

(A) the year 2000.

(B) the year 2062.

(C) the year 62.

(D) the year 1192.

2 Objective 1

The graph in this article is mainly about—

(A) using snow to make ice cream.

(B) vanilla ice cream.

(C) ice cream a long time ago.

(D) most liked ice cream in the U.S.

3 Objective 3

According to the chart which is the best selling ice cream?

(A) Butter Pecan

(B) Neapolitan

(C) Chocolate

(D) Vanilla

4 Objective 4

This author organizes the section after the first paragraph by using—

(A) a bar graph.

(B) number of people.

(C) names of companies.

(D) gallons.

USING YOUR NOODLE

Read the stories. Then use the power of logic to solve these tough problems.

Colorful Shoes

It is lunch time. Three friends are hanging out in the school yard. Each one wears sneakers of a different color. The boys' names are Billy, Steve, and Juan. The colors are black, orange, and green.

Billy is wearing black sneakers.

Steve is not wearing green sneakers.

1. What color sneakers is Steve wearing?

2. What color sneakers is Juan wearing?

Lunch Lesson

Alice, Tony, and Maxine all have cookies in their lunch boxes. One lunch box has 2 cookies in it. One lunch box has 3 cookies. And one lunch box has 4 cookies.

Maxine's lunch box has more than 3 cookies.

Tony's lunch box has the fewest cookies.

3. How many cookies are in Alice's lunch box?

4. How many cookies are in Tony's lunch box?

5. How many cookies are in Maxine's lunch box?

On Line

Three students are lined up. They are ready to enter school.

Mel stands behind Keisha.

Keisha stands behind Daryl.

6. Who stands in the front?

① Objective 1

This article is mainly about—

(A) shoes, lunch and lining up.

(B) things that happen at school.

(C) kinds of cookies.

(D) problems involving logic.

② Objective 2

In the first sentence, what does the word <u>tough</u> mean?

(A) nice

(B) sad

(C) hard

(D) easy

③ Objective 3

Look at the diagram below.

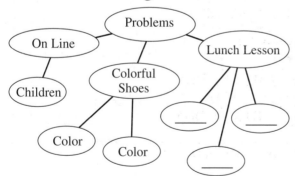

Which belongs in the blanks?
(A) Shoes
(B) Cookies
(C) Noodles
(D) Lessons

④ Objective 4

What did the author want the reader to use when he said "Using Your Noodle?"

(A) Use your brain.

(B) Use noodles.

(C) Use sneakers.

(D) Use children.

A Day at the Zoo

Read the story. Then solve the problems.

The Story:

¹   It's a nice day to head for the Children's Zoo. Timmy and Susie read the sign outside the zoo. It says the Children's Zoo opens at 10 o'clock in the morning. Inside the zoo, Timmy and Susie see another sign. It tells when the animals will be fed their meals. Here is what the sign says:

Feeding Schedule

At 11:25 the zookeepers will feed the birds fruits and worms.

At noon, apes will get their carrots.

At half past 12, the keepers will feed fish to the seals.

At 5 minutes to 1, the lions will be fed their lunch of meat and bones.

The Problems:

1. When does the Children's Zoo open?

2. Which animal has fish for lunch?

3. The last animals to eat are fed at what time?

4. How many minutes after the seals eat do the lions eat?

5. What time do the apes eat? Write it two different ways.

1 Objective 1

On the sign, what words help the reader know what the word <u>schedule</u> means?

(A) *zookeepers will feed*

(B) *apes will get their carrots*

(C) *lions will be fed their lunch*

(D) *11:25 noon, half past 12 and 5 minutes to 1*

2 Objective 2

According to the sign, who gets fed at 12:30?

(A) Susie

(B) Seals

(C) Timmy

(D) Birds

3 Objective 3

Look at the diagram below

Feeding Times

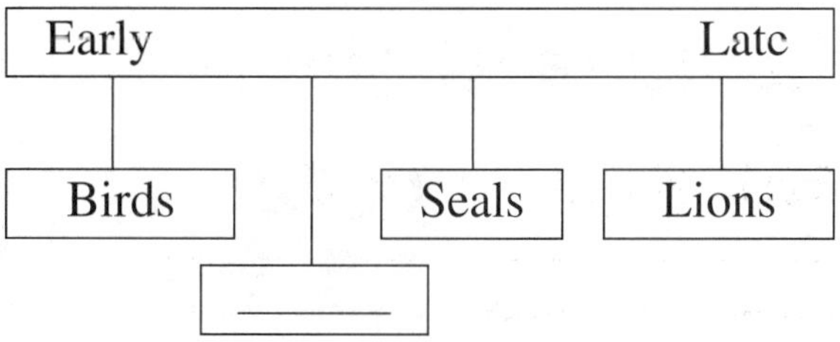

Early		Late

Birds	Seals	Lions

_____

Which idea belongs in the blank?

(A) Zoo

(B) Worms

(C) Apes

(D) Fish

4 Objective 4

Why does the author write the scheduled times differently?

(A) To give the reader practice reading all forms of time.

(B) To make the sentences longer.

(C) To add interest to the sign.

(D) To make sure visitors of the zoo wear a watch.

A Time Line of Toys

1   Toys and games have been popular for thousands of years. For example, people played with kites and yo-yos 1,000 years ago. This time line shows when some popular toys were first sold. The toys were invented many years ago. Children still play with them.

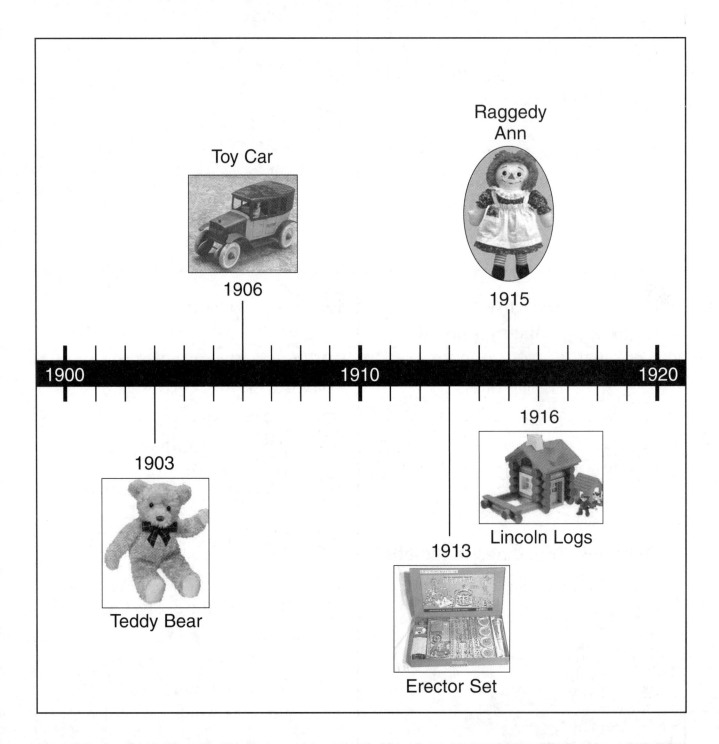

① **Objective 1**

According to the time line what was the first toy made?

Ⓐ Toy Car

Ⓑ Raggedy Ann

Ⓒ Lincoln Logs

Ⓓ Teddy Bear

② **Objective 1**

According to the time line when was the Erector Set invented?

Ⓐ 1903

Ⓑ 1906

Ⓒ 1913

Ⓓ 1915

③ **Objective 3**

Look at the diagram of information from the article

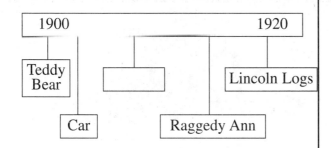

Which idea belongs in the box?

Ⓐ Erector Set

Ⓑ Kites

Ⓒ Yoyos

Ⓓ Play

④ **Objective 4**

What can the reader tell about older toys?

Ⓐ They are more fun.

Ⓑ They are more simple.

Ⓒ The are prettier.

Ⓓ They are more boring.

Discovered: Some Monster Planets!

It's a Strange Universe Out There

By Carlton Frisk

1   (SAN DIEGO, California, January 19.) For years, we Earthlings have known one thing about planets: There are nine of them, and they orbit our sun. But things have changed. Astronomers have found about 50 more planets since 1995. Most are very distant, very big, and very strange.

Weird Worlds

2   Recently, scientists found a very odd planet. Geoffrey Marcy is a planet hunter. He talked about two big discoveries at a meeting of astronomers in San Diego, California. The first discovery was a pair of giant planets. They are the size of Jupiter. (Jupiter is more than 1,000 times larger than Earth.) These planets move in a way that seems connected, like bicycle gears. They circle the same star. One planet takes 30 days to orbit its sun. The other planet takes exactly twice as long. No other planets orbit this way.

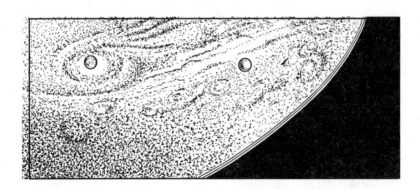

Planet or Star?

3   Marcy's second discovery was even stranger. He found a planet 17 times as massive as Jupiter. The planet was orbiting a very distant star. The planet is so big that Marcy calls it "frightening." Nobody knows if it is a planet or a star that's too small to shine, called a brown dwarf.

4   These and other odd discoveries have made scientists wonder: Are these planets weird? Or, is it our solar system that is weird?

1 Objective 1

According to this article Marcy is a planet hunter because—

Ⓐ he is an astronaut.

Ⓑ he has discovered new planets.

Ⓒ he went to a meeting.

Ⓓ he rides a bike.

2 Objective 1 (no obj 2)

In paragraph 1, the word Earthlings means—

Ⓐ people living on Earth.

Ⓑ worms living in Earth.

Ⓒ sounds coming from Earth.

Ⓓ rings around Earth.

3 Objective 3

Look at the diagram below.

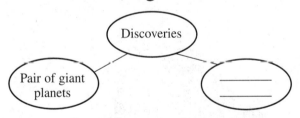

Which idea belongs in the blank?

Ⓐ One very, very small planet

Ⓑ Sun Spots

Ⓒ Jupiter's rings

Ⓓ One very, very large planet

4 Objective 4

What does the author mean by "Are these planets weird? Or, is it our solar system that is weird?"

Ⓐ Our solar system has all the aliens.

Ⓑ The large planets have all weird stuff.

Ⓒ Our solar system may be the system that is one of a kind.

Ⓓ The large planets have weird animals on them.

CHAPTER 4

Unit: Money and the Price of Things

Study This

When you pay for something, you want to use the fewest number of coins.

ALWAYS CHOOSE THE COIN WITH THE HIGHEST VALUE FIRST!

I'LL PAY FOR THE BALLONS WITH TWO QUARTERS AND A NICKEL. THAT MAKES 55 CENTS

You Do It

Pay for each item with the fewest number of coins. Tell the coins you choose.

4. DING-A-LING BROS. CIRCUS — 35¢

5. CIRCUS PROGRAM — 15¢

3.  POP CORN 45¢

1. 35¢

2. SIDESHOW 85¢

Important Words

penny—the smallest type of money, one cent; 1¢

nickel—the equal of five pennies; five cents; 5¢

dime—the equal of ten pennies or two nickels; ten cents; 10¢

quarter—one-fourth of a dollar; the equal of 25 pennies; 25 cents; 25¢

1 Objective 1

The article is mainly about—

(A) choosing something to buy with money you saved.

(B) paying with the fewest coins.

(C) going somewhere fun.

(D) how to study about money.

2 Objective 2

Where would someone most likely buy the things for sale on this page?

(A) at a toy store

(B) at a school

(C) at a circus

(D) at a church

3 Objective 3

Look at the web of information from the article

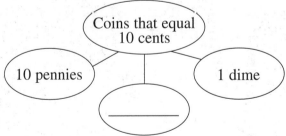

Which of these belongs in the empty oval?

(A) 2 nickels
(B) 2 dimes
(C) 2 quarters
(D) 1 dime and 1 nickel

4 Objective 4

The author organizes the last part of the article by—

(A) telling how to count coins.

(B) asking questions about money.

(C) explaining word problems.

(D) listing names and values of coins.

TABLE OF CONTENTS

A table of contents tells you where to look for the main subjects of a book. You can find the table of contents in the front of a book. Here is what a table of contents looks like in a math textbook.

Chapter 1:
Ways to Add and Subtract

Theme: At the Store
  A. Learning tips: addition. 1
  Practice 2
  Solving math story problems: making decisions 3
  Review 4
  B. Learning tips: subtraction . . . 5
  Practice 6
  Families of numbers: . . . . addition and subtraction 8
  Solving math story problems: reading with a purpose 9
  Review 11
Final Look
  Playing Games 12
  Extra Work 13
  Test 15
  How Did You Do? 16

Chapter 2:
How to Add 2-Digit Numbers

Theme: Fish in a Pond
  A. Learning tips: adding 2 digits without regrouping 18
  Practice 19
  Solving math story problems: ignoring extra data. 20
  Review 21
  B. Learning tips: knowing when you should regroup 22
  Practice 23
  Solving math story problems: using important data 24
  Review 25
Final Look
  Playing Games 26
  Extra Work 27
  Test 28
  How Did You Do? 29

❶ Objective 1

On which page in the book will you find tips for subtraction?

Ⓐ page 1

Ⓑ page 5

Ⓒ page 8

Ⓓ page 11

❷ Objective 3

The title of Chapter 1 is—

Ⓐ Math.

Ⓑ Table of Contents.

Ⓒ Ways to Add and Subtract.

Ⓓ How to Add 2-Digit Numbers.

❸ Objective 3

Read the outline of information from Chapter 1.

A. Learning Tips: Addition
• Practice
• _____
• Review

Which information belongs in the blank?

Ⓐ Solving math story problems: making decisions

Ⓑ At the Store

Ⓒ Playing Games

Ⓓ Extra Work

❹ Objective 4

Who would most likely use this book?

Ⓐ someone going shopping

Ⓑ someone going fishing in a pond

Ⓒ someone playing a game

Ⓓ someone in a math class

Want to travel by bus?
Then first look at a
schedule. It'll make
your trip a lot easier!

ROAD RUNNER BUS CO.

LEAVE **Mega City**	ARRIVE **Tiny Town**	ARRIVE **Crumbville**
Morning		
5:00	6:00	6:30
7:30	8:30	9:00
8:30	9:30	10:00
9:15	10:15	10:45
10:00	11:00	11:30
11:30	12:30	1:00
Afternoon/Evening		
12:30	1:30	2:00
3:00	4:00	4:30
6:20	7:20	7:50
8:45	9:45	10:15
10:00	11:00	11:30
11:30	12:30	1:00

- Tickets must by bought at the ticket window, not on the bus.

- The bus does not run on Thanksgiving and New Year's Day.

- There is no service to Crumbville on Sundays.

- There is no morning service to Tiny Town on holidays.

Thank you for choosing to travel on Road Runner!

① Objective 1

If a person leaves Mega City at 7:30, what time will the person get to Crumbville?

(A) 8:30

(B) 9:00

(C) 9:30

(D) 10:00

② Objective 2

Where can a person buy a bus ticket?

(A) in Tiny Town

(B) on the bus

(C) at the ticket window

(D) at RoadRunnerBus.com

③ Objective 3

If someone misses the 10:00 bus in Mega City, when does the next bus leave?

(A) 10:15

(B) 11:00

(C) 11:30

(D) 12:30

④ Objective 4

The author organizes the last part of the schedule by—

(A) listing information about going somewhere on the bus.

(B) telling rules for riding on a bus.

(C) listing times that the bus leaves each town.

(D) showing a map of where the bus goes.

Paid to Play Games

Do Athletes Make Too Much Money?

By Robert Sullivan

1   In 1930, New York Yankee Babe Ruth made $80,000. That year the President of the U.S. made $75,000.

2   Today the President makes $400,000 a year. And Alex Rodriguez of the Texas Rangers makes $25,200,000 a year. The two salaries are not in the same ballpark!

Earning Power

3   Today's athletes make a lot more money than presidents—and just about everybody else. For example, here are some different jobs and their average salaries: dentists ($106,000), mathematicians ($68,000), firefighters ($34,000), school bus drivers ($20,000), and farm workers ($17,000).

4   Compare those salaries to Shaquille O'Neal's salary. He makes $17,100,000 a year. Quarterback Bret Favre makes $10,000,000 a year. Why do athletes make so much money? Because fans buy millions of tickets to see them play.

Costly Tickets

5   As players salaries go up, so do ticket prices. A family of four can spend more than $250 to see a basketball game. They pay for tickets, food, parking, and so on. What happens if fewer fans buy tickets? The players will be paid less.

① Objective 1

Which of the following is the best summary of the article?

(A) Athletes get a lot of money. They make more than the president.

(B) Baseball players make more money than football payers. Basketball players make the least.

(C) Athletes get paid a lot more than most people. As their pay goes up, fans must pay a lot more, too.

(D) It is hard for a family to pay to go see a game. They could spend more than $250 at one game.

② Objective 1 (no obj 2)

How much money does the president make today?

(A) $75,000

(B) $80,000

(C) $400,000

(D) $25,200,000

③ Objective 3

Look at the diagram of information from the article.

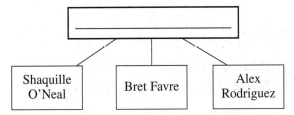

Which idea belongs in the empty box?

(A) People running for president

(B) High-paid athletes

(C) Members of the New York Yankees

(D) A dentist, a firefighter, and a farmer

④ Objective 4

What can the reader tell about the author?

(A) He thinks it costs too much to go to a basketball game.

(B) He wants to be an athlete.

(C) He thinks athletes need to make more money than they do.

(D) He goes to a lot of ball games.

THE BIG GAME

Read the information in the story. It will help you solve the problems.

The Story

1   Lots of people are gathered around the diamond. These baseball fans are watching the championship game.

2   The team on the field has four girls and five boys.

3   One team is beating the other 6 to 4.

4   The team that's ahead is called the Perry Street Pandas. The team that's winning is at bat.

5   There are 22 adults watching the game. There are also 17 kids watching the game.

The Problems

1. How many players are on the field?

2. How many runs have the Perry Street Pandas scored?

3. Does the story tell you the name of the team that is in the field?

4. Which team is at bat?

5. How many people are watching the game?

1 Objective 1

Read the meaning below for the word <u>diamond</u>.

> **diamond** (di´ mənd) *noun*
>
> **1.** a gem **2.** a shape **3.** a playing card **4.** a baseball field

Which meaning best fits the way <u>diamond</u> is used in the first paragraph?

(A) Meaning 1

(B) Meaning 2

(C) Meaning 3

(D) Meaning 4

2 Objective 3

What is the title of this article?

(A) *Math*

(B) *The Big Game*

(C) *The Story*

(D) *The Problems*

3 Objective 3

This article was mainly written to—

(A) explain how to play baseball.

(B) tell about two baseball teams.

(C) give math story problems about baseball.

(D) show readers how to throw a baseball.

4 Objective 4

What can the reader tell about the game?

(A) The score is close.

(B) The fans make a lot of noise.

(C) One team has girls and the other team has boys.

(D) Fans come to boo the other team.

Captain Bob's Seafood Restaurant

"We Serve Fish, Fish, and More Fish!"

Set Sail

Captain Bob's seafood salad. . $3.95
Fish sticks $2.95
Clam chowder. $3.50
Sardines on a stick $4.00

Something Fishy

Tuna salad sandwich. $4.95
Fried fish sandwich $5.95
Fish 'n' chips $6.50
Tuna melt. $5.25
Broiled lobster (1½ pound) . . $11.95
Fresh fish of the day: we grill it, bake it, fry it—your choice.
　　　　　　　　　Ask waiter for price.
Crab patty $9.95
Oysterburger with cheese $5.50
Spaghetti with clams $8.50

Drop Anchor

French fries $1.95
Cole slaw. $1.50
Potato salad $1.95
Rice. $1.75
Lemon slices . . . . $.95

Full Speed Ahead

Soft drinks $1.25
Coffee $1.50
Lemonade $1.95
Tea. $1.00
Milk . . . . $.95
Chocolate milk. $1.50
Fruit juice $1.25

1   **Objective 1**

According to the menu, which is the most expensive drink?

(A)   chocolate milk

(B)   crab patty

(C)   tea

(D)   lemonade

2   **Objective 3**

Look at the diagram of information from the article.

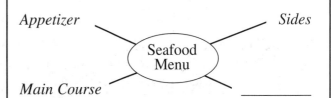

Which idea belongs in the blank?

(A)   *Drinks*

(B)   *Lobster*

(C)   *Fries*

(D)   *Salad*

3   **Objective 3**

If the restaurant owner adds onion rings to the menu, it would most likely be added under—

(A)   *Set Sail.*

(B)   *Something Fishy.*

(C)   *Drop Anchor.*

(D)   *Full Speed Ahead.*

4   **Objective 4**

Why does the menu NOT list the price of fresh fish of the day?

(A)   It is too expensive.

(B)   The price changes.

(C)   The menu was printed before the price was set.

(D)   The waiter wants to keep it a secret.

The Rising Price of Fuel

1 The price of oil is sky high. The high price is making it costly to drive cars and heat homes. Both gasoline and heating oil are made from crude oil. Not much crude oil is being produced. That means the price of crude oil will go up. If more crude oil is produced, its price will go down. Only a few nations produce oil. If they decide to pump more oil from their wells, the price will go down.

2 This graph shows the price of gasoline and heating oil for two years.

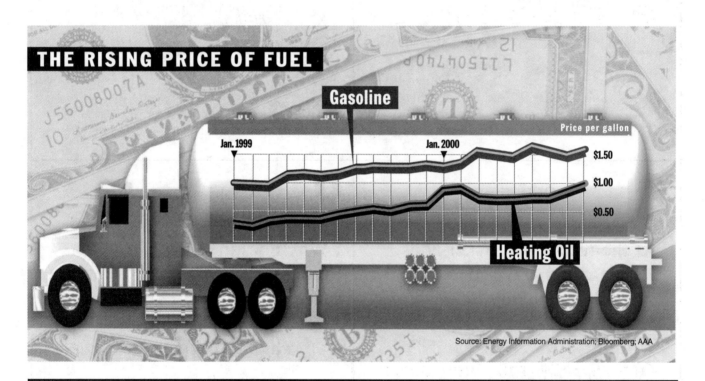

THE RISING PRICE OF FUEL

Gasoline

Heating Oil

Price per gallon

Jan. 1999 Jan. 2000

$1.50
$1.00
$0.50

Source: Energy Information Administration; Bloomberg; AAA

Your Turn

These questions are based on the graph.

1. Has the price of heating oil ever been more than the price of gasoline?

2. In 2000, did the price of heating oil always go up?

3. About how much more did gasoline cost than heating oil in January 1999?

4. Is $1.50 per gallon the most that gasoline cost in 2000?

1 Objective 1

According to the graph, the price of heating oil is—

Ⓐ   higher than gasoline.

Ⓑ   dropping.

Ⓒ   rising.

Ⓓ   less than 50 cents.

2 Objective 2

According to the article, why is the price of fuel rising?

Ⓐ   Iraq is holding back the oil.

Ⓑ   Not much crude oil is being produced.

Ⓒ   There are not enough trucks to carry the oil.

Ⓓ   People like to drive large cars.

3 Objective 3

Look at the diagram about the price of fuel.

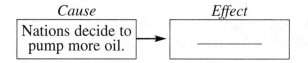

Cause — Nations decide to pump more oil.   →   *Effect* — _____

Which of the following goes in the blank?

Ⓐ   Prices will go down.

Ⓑ   Prices will stay the same.

Ⓒ   People will drive smaller cars.

Ⓓ   Nations will charge more for the oil.

4 Objective 4

Which sentence from the article shows the reader how rising fuel prices effect a family?

Ⓐ   *That means the price of crude oil will go up.*

Ⓑ   *This graph shows the price of gasoline and heating oil for two years.*

Ⓒ   *Both gasoline and heating oil are made from crude oil.*

Ⓓ   *The high price is making it costly to drive cars and heat homes.*

Sydney's Sewer Snapper

A Giant Turtle Surfaces After 20 Years

By Tabatha Cruz

1   If only this turtle could talk. Experts think it has been living under the streets of Sydney, Australia, for more than 20 years.

2   A construction worker found the rare alligator snapping turtle. It was in a Sydney sewer about 15 feet underground. "We couldn't believe our eyes," said the worker. "At first, it didn't look real." The turtle was 110 pounds. It took six men and a wheelbarrow to lift it from the drain.

An Old Story

3   This amazing turtle tale may have begun 21 years ago. That was when eight baby snappers were stolen from the Australian Reptile Park. They were never seen again. If this turtle is one of them, there could be seven more sewer turtles. In fact, there may be even more if the seven turtles have had families.

4   The alligator snapping turtles usually weigh around 200 pounds. They can also grow up to four feet long, including the tail.

5   These large freshwater turtles live to be 60 years old. So the Sydney turtle might live about 40 more years.

A Ninja turtle

6   The Sydney snapper has a nickname. It is called Leonardo. That is the name of one of the four cartoon Teenage Mutant Ninja Turtles.

7   The jumbo turtle now lives back home at the reptile park. Maybe one day Leonardo's brothers and sisters will join it at the park.

❶ Objective 1

Paragraph 6 is mostly about—

Ⓐ the Ninja Turtles.

Ⓑ the turtle's nickname.

Ⓒ a famous artist called Leonardo.

Ⓓ how long Leonardo has lived.

❷ Objective 2

Why hadn't Leonardo been found?

Ⓐ Rare alligator turtles can change colors and hide.

Ⓑ It was in Australia where few people ever go.

Ⓒ It was underground in a sewer.

Ⓓ It is so small, people couldn't see it.

❸ Objective 3

Read the chart below. It shows the order in which some events happened in the article.

Worker found the snapping turtle.

↓

They were amazed.

↓

_____

Which of these belongs in the empty box?

Ⓐ Eight baby snappers were stolen.

Ⓑ The sewer snapper was named Leonardo.

Ⓒ Six men and a wheelbarrow lifted the turtle.

Ⓓ The turtle lived at a reptile park.

❹ Objective 4

Which statement is true about Leonardo?

Ⓐ It hatched all alone.

Ⓑ There are many like it in the world.

Ⓒ It now lives in a special sewer.

Ⓓ It is still young.

The New Math: Problems, Problems

1   (CHICAGO, Illinois, March 12.) How should kids learn math? That's the question the National Council of Teachers of Mathematics is asking. Kids today do not learn math the same way their parents did. Years ago students had to memorize many math tables and rules. Now students explore math by solving problems, estimating, and using real-life experiences.

2   Kristine Hollod is a fourth-grade teacher. She says that even "kids who can't memorize" are able to do well in today's math.

Does It Work?

3   Does the new way of learning math work? Test scores show that kids are more creative in math than past students. But the tests also show a problem: Today's kids are doing badly on the kinds of math problems where memorizing is important.

4   Many experts believe that calculators are hurting math skills. Kids who use calculators don't always know the rules behind the math operations.

5   Math is giving many parents headaches. They don't always understand the new ways of learning it. They can't help their children study and do homework.

Solving the Problem

6   Some math teachers have a solution to these problems. They still want kids to use their imagination with math. But they also want students to memorize more math facts and rules. Said a member of the National Council of Teachers of Mathematics, "Knowing the addition facts, knowing the multiplication facts will make kids more comfortable with numbers."

① Objective 1

Read the meanings below for the word <u>table</u>.

table (ta´bǝl) *noun*

1. a piece of furniture **2.** the food and drink that is served at a meal **3.** a list of facts **4.** the people that get together for a meal

Which meaning best fits the way <u>table</u> is used in paragraph 1?

- Ⓐ Meaning 1
- Ⓑ Meaning 2
- Ⓒ Meaning 3
- Ⓓ Meaning 4

② Objective 2

What is the main problem in the article?

- Ⓐ Kids do not do well on math problems where they have to memorize.
- Ⓑ Parents do not know math as well as students.
- Ⓒ Calculators often break down during math class.
- Ⓓ Too many numbers are giving kids headaches.

③ Objective 3

This article was written mainly to—

- Ⓐ explain how playing with math is better than learning math facts.
- Ⓑ tell readers a funny math story.
- Ⓒ get readers to use calculators.
- Ⓓ tell about a problem in math and to present a solution.

④ Objective 4

Which sentence from the story shows the reader that teaching math has changed?

- Ⓐ *How should kids learn math?*
- Ⓑ *Kids today do not learn math the same way their parents did.*
- Ⓒ *Some math teachers have a solution to these problems.*
- Ⓓ *That's the question the National Council of Teachers of Mathematics is asking.*

A Sign of Hope

Brazil

Golden lion tamarins live in trees of the Atlantic Forest in Brazil.

1   A tiny monkey named Little Leon was just born in Brazil—the largest nation in South America. It was an exciting event! Little Leon is a golden lion tamarin. People have been working to save this kind of monkey because it is endangered. There are very few left in the world.

Good News

2   Little Leon is believed to be the 1,000th wild golden tamarin. These monkeys are the size of a squirrel. They live in the trees of the Atlantic Forest in Brazil. When trees are cut down, monkeys have fewer places to live. For many years researchers have been working to save tamarins and their rain forest homes. Their work is paying off.

3   This graph shows why there is hope for the golden tamarin monkeys.

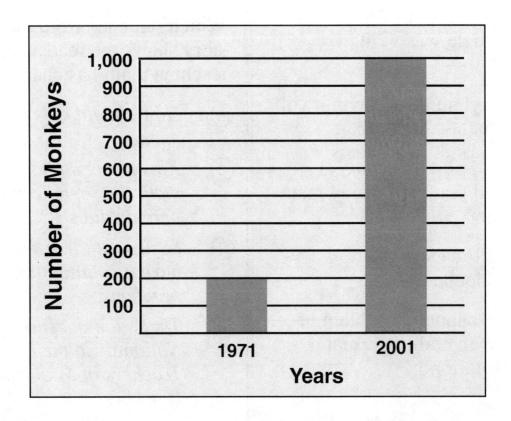

1   Objective 1

In paragraph 1, which words help the reader know what <u>endangered</u> means?

Ⓐ   *very few left*

Ⓑ   *kind of monkey*

Ⓒ   *in the world*

Ⓓ   *to save*

2   Objective 2

Which of these best describes the efforts of the researchers?

Ⓐ   amusing

Ⓑ   successful

Ⓒ   sad

Ⓓ   tiring

3 Objective 3

What is the title of this article?

Ⓐ   *Good News*

Ⓑ   *Number of Monkeys*

Ⓒ   *A Sign of Hope*

Ⓓ   *Math*

4   Objective 4

Why do researchers feel good about the tamarin monkey?

Ⓐ   The monkeys can take good care of themselves.

Ⓑ   The tamarins are living high up in trees.

Ⓒ   When trees are cut down, the tamarins move to other trees.

Ⓓ   The number of tamarins has grown.

Answer Key

Science

Page	
7	1. B, 2. D, 3. B, 4. C
9	1. D, 2. C, 3. B, 4. A
11	1. A, 2. C, 3. C, 4. D
13	1. C, 2. D, 3. A, 4. B
15	1. C, 2. B, 3. A, 4. D
17	1. B, 2. D, 3. C, 4. A
19	1. D, 2. A, 3. C, 4. A
21	1. B, 2. C, 3. A, 4. D
23	1. A, 2. B, 3. C, 4. D
25	1. C, 2. B, 3. B, 4. A
27	1. C, 2. A, 3. B, 4. D
29	1. B, 2. C, 3. A, 4. D
31	1. B, 2. D, 3. C, 4. A
33	1. C, 2. A, 3. B, 4. D
35	1. A, 2. A, 3. C, 4. D

Social Studies

Page	
37	1. B, 2. B, 3. D, 4. A
39	1. B, 2. D, 3. D, 4. A
41	1. D, 2. A, 3. A, 4. C
43	1. B, 2. A, 3. D, 4. C
45	1. D, 2. C, 3. C, 4. A
47	1. B, 2. A, 3. D, 4. C
49	1. D, 2. C, 3. B, 4. A
51	1. C, 2. D, 3. C, 4. B
53	1. B, 2. A, 3. C, 4. D
55	1. D, 2, B, 3. A, 4. C
57	1. B, 2. A, 3. D, 4. C
59	1. A, 2. C, 3. B, 4. D
61	1. C, 2. D, 3. B, 4. A
63	1. A, 2. D, 3. C, 4. B
65	1. C, 2. D, 3. B, 4. A

Answer Key (cont.)

	Language Arts		Math
Page		**Page**	
67	1. A, 2. A, 3. B, 4. D	97	1. C, 2. D, 3. D, 4. A
69	1. C, 2. D, 3. A, 4. B	99	1. D, 2. C, 3. B, 4. A
71	1. D, 2. B, 3. C, 4. A	101	1. D, 2. B, 3. C, 4. A
73	1. D, 2. B, 3. B, 4. A	103	1. D, 2. C, 3. A, 4. B
75	1. A, 2. C, 3. A, 4. B	105	1. B, 2. A, 3. D, 4. C
77	1. B. 2. B, 3. A, 4. D	107	1. B, 2. C, 3. A. 4. D
79	1. B, 2. A, 3. D, 4. C	109	1. B, 2. C, 3. A. 4. D
81	1. A, 2. B, 3. C, 4. D	111	1. B, 2. C, 3. C, 4. A
83	1. B, 2. C, 3. A, 4. C	113	1. C, 2. C, 3. B. 4. A
85	1. A, 2. D, 3. C, 4. B	115	1. D, 2. B. 3. C, 4. A
87	1. C, 2. A, 3. C, 4. D	117	1. D, 2. A. 3. C. 4. B
89	1. D, 2. D, 3. B, 4. A	119	1. C, 2. B, 3. A, 4. D
91	1. A, 2. B, 3. D, 4. C	121	1. B, 2. C, 3. C, 4. D
93	1. C, 2. A, 3. B, 4. C	123	1. C, 2. A, 3. D, 4. B
95	1. D, 2. B, 3. A, 4. B	125	1. A, 2. B, 3. C, 4. D